METACOGNITION IN THE PRIMARY CLASSROOM

Current trends in education suggest that pupils should have more responsibility for their own learning, but how can they if they don't understand the what, the why and the how?

This practical guide explores the idea that a metacognitive approach enables pupils to develop skills for lifelong learning. If pupils can identify the what, the why and the how of their learning, they can begin to formulate strategies for overcoming challenges and for continuous improvement.

In this book, the authors truly engage with research into the link between metacognition and learning, and the idea that if you can effectively articulate your thoughts and strategies regarding how you learn, you might then be in a better position to take actions in order to improve and to be able to learn best. Appendices of useful resources are also included, which offer a range of activities surrounding the language of learning, reflection and metacognition, as well as essential advice on how to develop metacognition in the early years (4–8), middle years (8–10) and upper years (10–13).

Metacognition in the Primary Classroom demonstrates how important it is for children to be sufficiently informed to play an active role in learning better. Having the language skills to talk about your learning, and the opportunity to share ideas and strategies with others, enables all concerned to explore and develop approaches in order to learn better. This book is a crucial read for anyone interested in ensuring that pupils take an active role in their own learning.

Peter Tarrant has been involved in teaching for 36 years and is a Senior Teaching Fellow in Initial Teacher Education at the University of Edinburgh, UK. He has been involved in a number of research projects involving topics such as teacher confidence and behaviour management, developing reflective practice and using a peer learning approach towards meta-cognitive practice.

Deborah Holt is Programme Director of the BEd Primary Education degree at the University of Edinburgh, UK. She was a primary school teacher and headteacher before moving into Initial Teacher Education. She has been working at Moray House since 2010 where she specialises in personal, social and emotional education and is currently undertaking research in this area for her doctorate.

METACOGNITION IN THE PRIMARY CLASSROOM

A practical guide to helping children understand how they learn best

Peter Tarrant and Deborah Holt

Routledge
Taylor & Francis Group

LONDON AND NEW YORK

First published 2016
by Routledge
2 Park Square, Milton Park, Abingdon, Oxon OX14 4RN

and by Routledge
711 Third Avenue, New York, NY 10017

Routledge is an imprint of the Taylor & Francis Group, an informa business

British Library Cataloguing in Publication Data
A catalogue record for this book is available from the British Library

Library of Congress Cataloging in Publication Data
Tarrant, Peter, author. | Holt, Deborah, author.
Metacognition in the primary classroom : a practical guide to helping children
understand how they learn best / Peter Tarrant and Deborah Holt.
Abingdon, Oxon ; New York, NY : Routledge, 2016.
LCCN 2015031880| ISBN 9781138842359 (hardback) | ISBN 9781315731636 (pbk.) |
ISBN 9781138842366 (ebook)
LCSH: Cognitive learning. | Metacognition in children. | Education, Elementary.
LCC LB1062 .T377 2016 | DDC 370.15/2--dc23LC record available at
http://lccn.loc.gov/2015031880

ISBN: 978-1-138-84235-9 (hbk)
ISBN: 978-1-138-84236-6 (pbk)
ISBN: 978-1-315-73163-6 (ebk)

Typeset in Interstate
by Cenveo Publisher Services

MIX
Paper from
responsible sources
FSC   FSC® C013056
www.fsc.org

Printed and bound in Great Britain by
TJ International Ltd, Padstow, Cornwall

CONTENTS

ACKNOWLEDGEMENTS

We would like to thank the following for their support, help and encouragement:

Anne Dobedoe
Sarah Sutcliffe
Caroline Findlay
Mandy McConnachie
Scott Lavery
Jennifer Allison
Cheryl Primrose
Carol-Ann Selfridge
Alison Herd

The Pupil Learning Council of the Lasswade ASG

Staff and pupils from the following Schools in Midlothian, Scotland:

Bonnyrigg Primary School
Burnbrae Primary School
Hawthornden Primary School
Lasswade Primary School
Loanhead Primary School
Paradykes Primary School
Rosewell Primary School
Roslin Primary School
Bilston Primary School

INTRODUCTION

This introductory chapter briefly discusses some of the work in schools in which the authors have been involved, as part of the background to writing. It explains the content and background to the rest of the book, giving suggestions on how to use the text and serving as a guide to the reader. The chapter makes clear the relevance of this text to other currently popular education texts and approaches.

For a number of years we have been interested in the learning processes that enable pupils to learn independently in school. In particular we have been engaged in research into the link between metacognition and learning. We are interested in the notion that if you can effectively articulate your thoughts and strategies regarding *how you learn*, you might then be in a better position to be able to take actions in order to improve and be able to learn *best*.

We have worked in many schools in Scotland and tried to find ways of enabling pupils to articulate their thoughts, feelings and strategies when it comes to learning.

This book is all about this approach: where having the language to talk about your learning and the opportunity to share ideas and strategies for learning with others enables all concerned to explore and develop their approaches in order to *learn better*.

In my book *Reflective Practice and Professional Development* (Tarrant 2013), I introduce some ideas for reflective monologues so that teachers can explore and articulate their reflections on their own practice in a setting, free from judgement and distraction. I also include a chapter suggesting how these *peer learning interactions* can be used with pupils in order to facilitate some reflection on how they learn.

This book takes this idea and develops it further. In our earlier research we taught pupils how to conduct a peer learning interaction. One pupil would take on the counsellor role and ask open questions such as:

Think of a lesson you have been in recently that sticks in your mind.
Tell me about that lesson; why was it memorable?
What kind of learning do you do?

> What did you do when you were stuck?
> How would you know if you did well or not?
> How could you have learned *better*?

The aim of the interaction would be for the person reflecting to have the opportunity to work it out for themselves: to think about what they learned and how they learned and to then think about how to move forward to become *better* at their learning.

However, in our early attempts to introduce this in schools we discovered that there was a fundamental problem with our idea. The children just did not have the vocabulary to talk about their learning in a meaningful way. If nobody had taught them how to talk about it, and if they hadn't been given many opportunities to do so, then the odds were against their being able to engage in productive and meaningful peer learning interactions.

Learning from this early experience, when invited to work on developing a metacognitive approach in another school, we began by introducing the language of learning. We taught the staff to use the language in their lessons. We made the thinking and learning process much more explicit. We began to model how one might approach a new problem, or an old one that had proved to be tricky in the past. Eventually we began to introduce the peer learning interactions; this time, with much more success. The children were able to sustain a conversation about their learning and come to some realistic and practical suggestions about how to learn better. In this book, you will find details and suggestions for facilitating learning conversations in your own school or class.

In Chapter 1 there is more detail on exactly what metacognition in the primary classroom actually looks like. We explore some of the key literature on this approach and consider some of the evidence to suggest that a metacognitive approach is beneficial to learning. In addition to the many chapters that offer practical advice on how to develop this approach in the school or classroom, we also use examples from practice throughout the book to illustrate the points that we make.

Chapter 2 deals with introducing the language of learning and suggests ways in which you might go about this. Chapter 3 explores ways of getting the dialogue going and preparing for peer learning interactions. Chapters 5–8 look at ways of introducing a metacognitive approach to learning in the nursery and reception (Chapter 5), the early years (Chapter 6), the middle school years (Chapter 7) and the upper years of primary school (Chapter 8). At the end of this introduction Table 0.2 shows where in the practical chapters key metacognitive language is used. In Chapter 9 we consider how this approach would look if it were introduced throughout the school. Finally in Chapter 10 we consider the impact on learning and explore how we enable the pupils to become *better learners*.

The book is aimed at teachers, students and headteachers. The goal is to have all pupils engaged in thinking and talking about how they learn and exploring ways of learning best.

We hope that this will be a practical guide, backed by some recent theory and research. At the back of the book there are ideas and resources that should support you in getting started, whether you are an experienced teacher, a student just at the early stage of your career, or a headteacher planning to launch a metacognitive initiative in your school.

Currently in schools in Scotland there is an interest in using Bloom's (1956) taxonomy to develop metacognition through his questioning approach. There is also interest in the mind-set work of Carol Dweck (2012), and this has had some impact on schools with the focus being switched from what we learn to how we learn. Work from John Hattie (2011) has also been used to get teachers talking and thinking about the learning process.

This text tries to link these elements together into a practical resource that will explain the theory and the process and support educators in their first steps to introducing this process-focused approach into their own schools and classrooms.

Metacognitive approaches towards Bloom's taxonomy

Bloom's (1956) taxonomy is a tool that can currently be found in many classrooms (see Table 0.1). It is used to access the learning process and to structure questioning. It is important to consider, however, whether all the children have a shared understanding of what the taxonomy words displayed in their classrooms actually mean.

Using a metacognitive approach we can select each word and unpack it, exploring what it means in each individual context. In this way, pupils can begin to develop the vocabulary to explore and describe *how they learn best*.

One approach might be:
I know I can *remember* what I have learned because

- I can describe the details of what I know;
- I can name them;
- I can make a list of them.

I know I can *understand* something I have learned because I can

- explain this to a partner or an audience;
- compare this to other learning;
- discuss what I remember and what I think about it;
- predict what might happen in another context using my knowledge here.

This is a good way to start. However, it might mean more to the pupils, and provide more ownership of this learning, if they are then asked to provide their own ideas for each word, i.e. make a list of ways you might demonstrate that you can

- apply your knowledge of this learning;
- analyse this information;
- evaluate this learning.

Table 0.1 Bloom's taxonomy

Remember	Understand	Apply	Analyse	Evaluate	Create
describe	explain	complete	compare	justify	plan
name	compare	use	contrast	assess	invent
find	discuss	examine	examine	prioritise	compose
list	predict	illustrate	identify	recommend	design
relate	outline	classify	categorise	rate	construct
find	restate	solve	investigate	decide	imagine

By including the learners in a metacognitive conversation, where they need to think about how they learn, they will develop a much more heightened understanding of what learning is.

Clearly many of the words in this taxonomy are used throughout this book. There are examples of how some of them might be profiled incidentally or specifically in lessons, and there are ideas for taking a whole school focus on one word and ensuring a shared understanding.

It is recommended that you read the first few chapters of this book to get an understanding of the *what* and the *why* of the metacognitive approach. Thereafter you can select the chapter that has most relevance to where in the school you will be teaching. It is worth having a look at the other practical chapters (5-8) as each contains ideas and activities that can be adapted for use with children of other ages.

As this book is designed so that the reader can select the sections they think are most appropriate for their purpose, there is a revisiting of key ideas throughout the book, as we explore from a range of different perspectives key concepts such as the language of learning and how to embed it, reflection and creating an environment for metacognition.

Each chapter also provides some suggestions for things to think about or activities that you might go away to try before moving on to the next chapter. At the end of Chapters 5–8 you will find a table of the learning processes that have been discussed as a record and inspiration for your own work in class. Table 0.2 below provides a quick guide to where these terms and processes are exemplified in Chapters 5–8. If you would like to look at how this language and these processes can be incorporated into teaching, you may wish to look at the case studies in the practical chapters.

Table 0.2 Guide to locating key metacognitive processes in the case studies

Process	Chapter 5 Case Study	Chapter 6 Case Study	Chapter 7 Case Study	Chapter 8 Case Study
applying experience or learning			1, 2, 3, 4	1, 4
being a good team member		5	3	
checking			2	
choosing/deciding	3, 4	1, 3, 4, 5	1, 2, 3, 4	2, 4
concentrating			2	
considering others			1, 3	4
cooperating		5		2, 3, 4
explaining		2, 3, 5		5
exploring		3, 5	2, 3	
expressing/explaining feelings and thoughts			1, 3, 4	5
feeling	1	4		
finding/looking for evidence				5
justifying predictions or decisions			2, 4	5
keep trying	1, 2	5		
listening		1, 5	3, 4	2, 3
listening to the opinions of others			1, 2, 3, 4	
looking	1	1, 2, 5		1, 3, 5
looking for patterns			3	5
making connections			1, 2, 3, 4	1, 3, 4, 5
noticing/observing			2	
planning			2, 3	2, 4
predicting				2
redrafting, revising, improving			1, 3	2, 3, 4
remembering	3	1, 2, 4		
remembering other learning		1, 3, 5	1, 2, 3, 4	2, 3
sharing	2, 3	3, 4		

Table 0.2 Guide to locating key metacognitive processes in the case studies (continued)

Process	Chapter 5 Case Study	Chapter 6 Case Study	Chapter 7 Case Study	Chapter 8 Case Study
showing others		3		
solving problems		2, 5	2	1
suggesting		5		
taking turns	2	3		
testing		2, 5	1, 2, 3	
thinking	1, 3	1, 2, 4, 5	1, 2, 3, 4	1, 2, 3
trying different ways		2, 3, 5		
trying out/finding out (having a go/guess)	1	1, 5	1, 2, 3	1, 3
using imagination	3	3, 4		5
wondering	1	4, 5		
working out		1, 5	2, 3, 4	1, 2, 3, 5

References

Bloom, B. S. (ed.) (1956) *Taxonomy of Educational Objectives: The Classification of Educational Goals, Handbook 1.* London: Longman.

Dweck, C. (2012) *Mindset: How You Can Fulfil Your Potential.* New York: Ballantine Books.

Hattie, J. (2011) *Visible Learning for Teachers: Maximizing Impact on Learning.* London: Routledge.

Tarrant, P. (2013) *Reflective Practice and Professional Development.* London: SAGE.

1 What and why
A look at theory and rationale

This chapter seeks to answer the following question: What is metacognition and why is it worth investing time and energy in developing metacognitive skills in children when there are so many other pressures in the primary classroom? The chapter starts with a definition of metacognition, drawing from some of the key literature in the field. Reference to classroom practice is used to illustrate what the theory actually might look like in practice. This is followed by discussion of the benefits of metacognition to the child, the teacher and the school as a whole.

Introduction - What is metacognition?

Metacognition is the knowledge of cognitive processes (Galton 2006). Metacognitive knowledge is defined as what we know about ourselves as a thinker and learner. It is important in education because such self-knowledge can be used not only to inform and support action, but also because it underpins our concept and identity as a thinker and a learner (Desautel 2009).

In the classroom, metacognitive knowledge equates to the children knowing themselves as learners; having an understanding of how they learn; and being more aware of the processes and actions that they use during learning or to achieve the learning outcome of a lesson. This book works on the premise that understanding how they learn helps a child to be able to learn better, particularly, but not only, if they face a challenge.

The benefits to pupils will be discussed in more detail later, but it is helpful at this point to explain in what way a metacognitive approach can support learning. Making explicit what is actually going on during a learning activity can help deepen the understanding of the intended learning, making it more secure. For example, it may help a child who struggles to sort and classify materials in science or shapes or numbers in maths to understand exactly what processes are involved in sorting. To the unaware, sorting and classifying may look like some magic, rather random process that goes on inside someone's head. Taking a metacognitive approach to sorting and classifying would involve breaking down the process to find out the unobservable steps. The stages in sorting and classifying are often part of a sequence of lessons in the primary classroom, but does the teacher always help the children to see the relevance of these stages and how they support classification? The children are faced with a series of materials that they have to sort according to a chosen criterion. The first step is to look carefully and observe the features of the materials. The children may also use other senses to explore. It is helpful if they are encouraged to voice the features identified. They might touch or smell them, for example, and say, 'It feels rough. It smells like the sea'. The children need to be aware that they are *looking carefully*, *using their senses*, *describing* or *explaining*. The next step in sorting is to *compare* or look for similarities and differences in these features. They will need to *think* carefully, often they will have to *remember prior learning* or, if classifying, look up and *find out* the criteria for a particular material, shape or set of numbers - such as *checking* what a makes a prime number. They then have to *decide* which of these to use as their criteria for sorting. In summary, in those often brief moments between being given a set of objects to sort and the final set of groupings, a child will

- observe;
- use their sense to explore;
- identify the features;
- think;
- remember other learning;
- sometimes check information or find out more;
- choose how to sort - which features or characteristics to use.

Afterwards they will be expected to

- explain their thinking;
- justify their choice.

Metacognition in the primary classroom involves placing emphasis on these many and often hidden processes, making them more explicit for the child. In this way, the child is finding out about how they learn in such a way that it will also support future learning. Chapter 6 explains how activities involving sorting can be used as a route into developing metacognition.

In becoming more aware of the 'how' of learning, pupils can then see that they do not always learn in the same way and that different lessons, disciplines or activities might require a different set of skills. They will also discover which learning processes and skills they do well and those in which they have more difficulty or less enthusiasm.

Whilst there may be similarities between the skill sets and processes involved in different areas of the primary curriculum, there are also transferable skills. As a child begins to become more aware of how they learn best, they should be able to transfer a skill from one subject area in which they feel confident, such as maths, to another in which they struggle. For example, they might be aware that when solving a maths problem they may try out one way, consider the sense or *check* their work and then *try again in a different way*. Such an approach might also support them in their writing. They might realise that it is okay to *try* writing a sentence or paragraph, reread to *check* the writing and then *have another go* (or *redraft*) if it is not what they wanted. Learning that trial and error, trying out different ways, checking and revisiting are skills used across learning can increase their competence as a learner.

Chapters 5–8 explore age-specific approaches to embedding metacognition into daily classroom practice. Metacognitive ability changes with age (Flavell *et al.* 1995). However, these chapters can be used flexibly as metacognitive skills may depend more on experience than age, making the teacher's role crucial to the process (Fisher 1995). For this reason, the introductory metacognition lesson 'Guess My Rule', included in Chapter 6, could be used with children of any age. An explicit focus on metacognition by the teacher is required in order to raise awareness and metacognitive ability levels in their pupils. This is discussed further in Chapter 2.

Metacognition in the primary classroom

It is argued that an integral part of a teacher's role is to provide children with the opportunities to talk and think about their learning (Alexander 2004; Bruner 1960). Talk in the classroom should be valued by teachers, for its own merit and for the opportunity to develop the thinking that arises when talking about learning: 'The construction of knowledge requires that people put some things into words ... so that they can be shared' (Mercer 1995: 67). Once a child begins to put thoughts into words, the teacher can see what is going on for that child, what they are doing and how they are doing it. The teacher can model and support this process by using 'think alouds' in which the thoughts are voiced.

> For example when spelling a word, the teacher could voice some of the thinking a child might be doing. 'How do I spell shine? I know it begins with a *sh*. I also need an eye sound, I think that means using a magic *e*. *Sh* and then *in* with *e* makes an eye sound. S H I N E.'

Not only does the voicing of thoughts enhance learning, but once voiced these thoughts are visible to the teacher who can use this knowledge to support and further learning: 'practical hands-on activity can gain new depths of meaning if it is talked about' (Mercer 1995: 13). This book works on the premise that through talking about the process of learning children will not only become more aware of themselves as learners, better able to self-evaluate, but they will also deepen their understanding of what they have been learning. In this way, they take greater ownership of their learning which, it can be argued, is the key to success: 'The goal of education ... is the facilitation of change and learning. The only person who is educated is the person who has learned how to learn' (Freiberg and Rogers 1990: 104).

Much has been written about metacognition and the significance of 'thinking about thinking' (Flavell 1979). A wide body of literature supports the view that there is value in making the processes of learning more explicit. Fisher (1995) summarises a number of 'teaching to learn' cognitive strategies identified in recent research, including 'discussing' and 'co-operative learning', as among those that help develop metacognition. Feuerstein (1980) shows how adults can play a key role in encouraging this awareness in children. Nisbet and Shucksmith (1986) talk of a set of six strategies for successful learning which involve asking questions, planning, monitoring, checking, revising and self-testing. However, 'thinking about thinking' is not enough. Learning depends on conversations, on the negotiation of personal meanings through dialogue with others, leading to understanding (Harri-Augstein and Thomas 1991). The approach to metacognition advocated in this book is intended to make the language of learning an explicit and established part of classroom practice, with an emphasis on how children learn embedded in the planning.

The aim of this book is to support children not only to talk about their learning in appropriate language but to have a deeper understanding of the many and varied ways in which they learn. The combination of dialogue and metacognition should result in rich effective learning conversations and children who understand not only *what* but *how* they learn.

> Language and thought are intimately related, and the extent and manner of children's cognitive development depend to a considerable degree on the forms and contexts of language which they have encountered and used.
>
> (Alexander 2004: 18)

The subsequent chapters in this book will go into greater detail on how the primary class teacher can support pupils' metacognitive development. Before that, we will take a closer look at why a metacognitive approach is beneficial to learning in the primary school.

Benefits for the pupils

Metacognition is about the *how* of learning rather than the *what*. Children often talk about what they did. An emphasis on *how* they achieved the lesson outcomes or *how* they approached the task puts the emphasis back onto the child as a learner. It helps them to learn about themselves as a learner whilst also developing the intended skills, attitudes and conceptual knowledge of a lesson. Such metacognitive awareness can only help them to be better at learning. Knowledge of how they learn and the understanding of the thought processes in which they engage allow the children eventually to become 'professional learners' who think and act as learners (Galton 2006; Lahelma and Gordon 1997).

As we shall explain in Chapter 2 'The Language of Learning', in order to move from talking about *what* they do to being able to discuss *how* they work children need to develop a learning vocabulary so that they have the language of learning. Being able to articulate their thinking and engage in discussion about learning is of benefit to the children, providing an important foundation on which they can build during their secondary school education and without which, according to Sammons *et al.* (1995), they will have a serious handicap. Self-evaluation is an important skill in the workplace and in all learning. Having the tools to make learning more visible and more readily articulated will enable pupils to develop this essential transferable life skill.

As children develop a greater understanding of how they learn and begin to apply this knowledge to other learning, their self-esteem can be improved and barriers to learning can sometimes be identified and overcome. In Chapters 6 and 7 we talk about transferable skills and how to make a child aware of the transferability of skills they are using in a specific lesson. When a child becomes aware that they have the ability to persevere, solve problems, concentrate and try different ways in a sports activity or a console game they may then have the confidence to apply these skills in other settings. For example, Kirsty always panicked when it came to maths. The shutters came down and she was overwhelmed with the feeling of 'I can't do it'. A focus on the skills and processes involved in maths and a consideration of other parts of the curriculum where she actually exhibited these skills and engaged in these processes with confidence helped to remove Kirsty's almost irrational feelings of inadequacy in maths.

It is also helpful for the teacher to be aware that the child has such skills in other contexts so that they can set appropriate expectations and remind the child of their strengths. Sometimes more able pupils can have an almost disabling shock when they first encounter something that they do not immediately find easy. If they are able to work out what processes are required for the task, they will be better able to overcome the challenge. They or the teacher may then also identify that the child compensates for a weakness or lack of experience in some skills by using others. An example of this might be a child who has a good visual memory, resulting in a high number of words that they can read on sight. At some point the child encounters tricky words in their reading that they cannot read or spell. They will need to switch from *remembering* and draw on other learning processes such as using phonic knowledge (*using other learning*), *trying out*, reading on for meaning and *considering the sense* etc.

Pupils can use metacognitive knowledge about themselves to make choices about their learning and to support their learning. They understand how they learn and use this knowledge to learn better. It is therefore no surprise that in Scotland the use of such knowledge actually falls within the curriculum area of Health and Wellbeing (personal, social and emotional education). 'Through taking part in a variety of events and activities, I am learning to recognise my own skills and abilities as well as those of others' (Scottish Executive 2010: n.p.).

Benefits for the teacher

Experienced teachers were interviewed in order to evaluate the impact on their work of introducing a focus on talking about learning. They cited as a benefit that taking a metacognitive approach in the classroom had helped them to keep a sharper focus on learning processes when planning. Making a note of the learning processes in daily or weekly plans made teachers aware of any specific learning approaches or skills that were being used too often or not often enough (Holt and Tarrant 2012). It is important to plan to ensure that children experience the range of learning processes and skills during their working week. Chapters 5–8 give suggestions on how this might be done and the appendices also include tools to support a systematic approach to metacognition.

As the children develop the language in which to talk about their learning, the teacher can get greater insight into each child as a learner. Such insight can inform planning for differentiation and the mix of approaches and teaching strategies employed.

Some of the tools for supporting metacognition can be used to record pupil progress and achievement. In addition to this, the knowledge that both teacher and pupil gain through the deeper understanding of learning can feed into or underpin class and individual assessment record systems such as Personal Development Portfolios (PDPs), learning profiles or journals. As the pupils use their metacognitive knowledge to become better at self-evaluation and to engage in dialogue about their learning with peers and teachers, this will support the teacher to meet their responsibility to demonstrate knowledge of individual pupil progress.

Ultimately the potential benefit to the teacher of an embedded metacognitive approach is that there is a culture of learning, and talking about learning, in the classroom. This culture will support pupils to achieve their potential as learners and to tackle the new and the challenging. Furthermore it will help pupils to have a secure understanding of the many ways in which they learn, and how they might learn even better.

Benefits for the whole school

A metacognitive approach develops pupils' understanding of themselves as learners. This is crucial to the process of self-evaluation, a key part of current education policy all over the world. Children who understand how they learn and who can engage in discussion about their learning are better able to identify their strengths and development needs as a learner. As a result, they will be in a much stronger position to take responsibility for their own learning, set personal targets and evaluate their progress towards these targets. Metacognitive knowledge of self as a learner can increase feelings of self-efficacy, allowing children to be more independent as learners, whilst also knowing when and how to seek help and overcome challenges in learning. Research has found that after an increased emphasis on metacognition had been incorporated into the classroom, pupils' responses to the question 'What do you do when you are stuck?' changed significantly. They moved from predominantly saying that they would ask the teacher to suggesting strategies such as trying another way, thinking about it, checking, talking (Holt and Tarrant 2012).

In summary, a metacognitive approach

- develops metacognitive knowledge – children understand how they learn so that they are able to learn better;
- enables children to use metacognitive knowledge to overcome difficulties;
- supports self and peer-assessment;
- develops independence in learners' ownership of own learning;
- fits with a culture of 'trying' and 'it's okay to have a go' and 'it's okay to make a mistake', as multiple approaches to one task are recognised;
- maintains the focus on planning around how children learn, putting the emphasis on process rather than product;
- gives teachers insight into how individual children learn, so informing planning, differentiation and choice of approach;
- enhances ability to talk about learning, engage in dialogue, listening skills and collaboration;
- contributes to social and emotional development;
- supports development of personal learning records/PDPs.

Summary and key points

This chapter is intended to serve as a small literature review of this topic and considers some of the key literature underpinning a metacognitive approach. The term 'metacognition' is defined and examples from primary school practice are used to illustrate how this approach can be put into practice and what it might involve for teachers and children.

The chapter then identifies the benefits of taking this metacognitive approach for the pupils, the teacher and for the whole school. The chapter concludes with a summary of the key features.

Next steps for the reader

- We recommend that you consider what is said here in relation to your context.
- Can you visualise such an approach? How does it fit in with what you are already doing?
- Read some of the other chapters in the book and revisit this chapter to consolidate understanding.
- You may wish to read some of the texts cited.

References

Alexander, R. (2004) *Towards Dialogic Teaching: Rethinking Classroom Talk*. York: Dialogos.

Bruner, J. (1960) *The Process of Education*. Cambridge MA: Harvard University Press.

Desautel, D. (2009) Becoming a Thinking Thinker: Metacognition, Self-Reflection, and Classroom Practice. *Teachers College Record*, 111(8): 1997-2020.

Feuerstein, R. (1980) *Instrumental Enrichment: An Intervention Program for Cognitive Modifiability*. Glenview, IL: Scott Foresman & Company.

Fisher, R. (1995) *Teaching Children to Learn*. Cheltenham: Stanley Thornes.

Flavell, J. H. (1979) Metacognition and Cognitive Monitoring: A New Area of Cognitive-Development Inquiry. *American Psychologist*, 34: 906-11.

Flavell, J., Green, F. and Flavell, E. (1995) Young Children's Knowledge About Thinking. *Monographs for the Society for Research in Child Development*, 60(1): i-113.

Frieberg, J. and Rogers, C. (1990) *Freedom to Learn*. New York: Merrill.

Galton, M. J. (2006) *Learning and Teaching in the Primary Classroom*. London: SAGE.

Harri-Augstein, S. and Thomas, L. (1991) *Learning Conversations*. London: Routledge.

Holt, D. and Tarrant, P. (2012) Talking to Learn and Metacogniton. Paper presented at the annual Scottish Education Research Association conference at the University of West Scotland Ayr Campus, 21-23 November.

Lahelma, E. and Gordon, T. (1997) First Day in Secondary School: Learning to Be a Professional Pupil. *Educational Research and Evaluation*, 2: 119-39.

Mercer, N. (1995) *The Guided Construct of Knowledge*. Clevedon: Multilingual Matters.

Nisbet, J. and Shucksmith, J. (1986) *Learning Strategies*. London: Routledge.

Sammons, P., Hillman, J. and Mortimer, P. (1995) Key Characteristics of Effective Schools: A Review of School Effectiveness Research. Paper presented at an internal seminar for Ofsted, Institute of Education, London, March.

Scottish Executive (2010) *Curriculum for Excellence: Health and Wellbeing Experiences and Outcomes*. Livingston: Scottish Executive.

2 The language of learning

This chapter has as its focus the language of learning and seeks to answer the question: How do we support the development of the appropriate vocabulary so that pupils are empowered to use it to articulate their thinking about how they learn (*best*)? The chapter explores what is meant by the language of learning, identifies some key vocabulary necessary for the articulation of learning and discusses how this can be introduced and embedded into classroom life. We explain how development of the vocabulary is crucial to a metacognitive approach as it provides a shared language in which pupils can communicate their thinking and learning processes.

Introduction

- What does the phrase 'language of learning' mean?
- Why is it important?
- How do we introduce and model the language of learning?
- How do we support the development of the appropriate vocabulary so that pupils are able to articulate their thinking about how they learn?

When thinking and talking about our learning and how we learn best it is important to consider the words available for describing how we learn. Such words are not necessarily already present in the vocabulary of the learners; they have to be taught, made explicit, modelled and reinforced. Whether you are adopting this meta-learning approach for the first time or are building upon work done by the pupils in your school in recent years, many of the strategies and milestones are the same. It might be that you are merely revisiting and consolidating learning and language that has been covered before or that you are starting from scratch. Either way, the different phases should be visited and developed.

Below we discuss these phases and some things that you might do in class. Although you might do different activities depending on where you are in the school, the same basic principles will still apply.

Let us now investigate the different phases of introducing and developing the language of learning in the classroom:

- Phase 1: Heightening awareness
- Phase 2: Immersion in the language
- Phase 3: The metacognitive language cycle
- Phase 4: Reflection on how we learn

Phase 1: Heightening awareness

Metacognition is about heightened awareness of learning.

> 'Teaching the children the words has made a big difference because the words that describe the way they learn help them be aware of the methods they use.' (Miss Cameron, Roslin Primary)

It is possible for a child to be aware of how they learn, but if they do not have the language of learning they cannot communicate this knowledge. In the classroom we need a shared understanding of the language of learning so that we can introduce and develop strategies for helping children to talk about how they learn and to think about how they learn better. The first phase should involve some ways of heightening their awareness of this language and to realise that this is an important tool for learning how to learn.

First we need to heighten awareness of the thinking processes. What is actually going on when pupils are making choices about learning? When we are learning there is often lots going on in our heads that we might not realise. We might be applying reasoning processes and thinking strategies without being aware of what we are doing. If we can identify these approaches and make them more explicit we might be able to support and develop the capacity for some pupils to learn better.

What do we mean here? When we first began to work on talking about learning with primary pupils (10-year-olds), we encouraged them to talk about their learning; but we quickly found that they only thought about learning in terms of *hard/easy*, *liking/disliking* and *what the teacher said*. They needed a great deal of encouragement to consider and then name the actual processes in which they were engaged. This awareness can be raised by a teacher's use of appropriate language such as: *wondering*, *thinking*, *exploring*, *testing*, while modelling or making such processes explicit to the children. The children will begin to see similar processes in different subject areas and have a greater understanding of what they are doing, what they find difficult and what they might do differently. They will begin to see connections between the kinds of thinking in different activities and subject areas and to become aware that they are transferable. Such skills are essential for successful lifelong learning.

Word banks

Below is a list of some of the things that we might need to do before, during or after a learning activity or experience. Such a word bank can be useful for articulating what it is we do when we learn. (See Appendix 1 for copies of this and other related resources.)

wondering	exploring	thinking	testing	trying out
guessing	choosing	deciding	suggesting	estimating

trying	thinking	concentrating	taking care	using a plan
working out	problem-solving	trying different ways	making connections	remembering other learning

remembering	checking	considering	noticing	improving
redrafting	showing others	adding more detail	making changes	making connections

This awareness of the thinking processes can be helpful to all pupils. For example: the child who was very able at aspects of number work but lost his confidence when he struggled with shape and measure. He was used to doing well in maths yet he found this new area challenging. He could see that working with shape and measure was different but was not confident that he had the tools to do so successfully. The shape and measure topic required *careful observation, estimation, knowledge of shape terminology and the properties of shape*, processes with which he was not confident.

Following consideration and identification of the skills and processes involved in these branches of maths, he came to see that the ways of learning with which he engaged so confidently and successfully in other areas of maths such as *making connections, seeing patterns, trying different ways, solving problems*, were also relevant to his shape and measure work.

He was then able to talk about the skills that he needed to develop to be as strong in shape and measure as he was in his number work: he had a better idea of what it actually was that he found hard and the confidence regained from knowing this, alongside his awareness that he still had some skills to bring to the task, made a real difference to his attitude and approach.

In the case study below we show how a learning conversation with a child or group can encourage them to articulate their thinking and help tease out the learning processes taking place.

Case Study 1: Naming a process

A simple example of the benefits of heightening awareness might be a 'what comes next?' problem in maths. The child has been learning about shapes and pattern. S/he is given a sequence of shapes and are asked to use their knowledge of shape to work out what comes next in the sequence.

Teacher:	Look at the different shapes and decide what comes next in the sequence.
Child:	I think it will be the triangle because ....
Teacher:	How do you know?
Child:	It has three sides.

Teacher:	Is that important in this pattern?
Child:	Yes. I *guessed* the rule was the number of sides: five sides, four sides, three sides, five sides, four sides, three sides.
Teacher:	What did you do first?
Child:	I *looked* and I *counted* how many sides the shapes had and I *knew* that the next shape needed to have three sides so it has to be a triangle. I know that triangles have three sides.
Teacher:	So what would come after the triangle?

Analysis

In this example, the child benefits from being aware of and naming the processes within this problem. What are they doing to solve the problem? They might be looking for patterns, making connections, applying this new knowledge of the pattern or connection to work out what comes next. In this case, the child got far more than being able to solve the problem; in explaining how they solved it, they became more aware of all the steps that they took: their thought process became explicit. This identification and naming of the process can deepen the learning about how to solve such problems so that the child is better able to apply the same skills in another context.

> Language is therefore not just a means by which individuals can formulate ideas and communicate them, it is also a means for people to think and learn together.
>
> (Mercer 1995: 4)

This is a transferable skill that they might apply in another context but it is the articulation of that process that helps to consolidate it in their minds.

Additionally, if a child experiencing difficulty with a problem can name the steps or processes they have taken, their teacher will be better able to support them to overcome difficulties in solving the problem. Moreover, the child will have the vocabulary to describe how they might tackle a similar problem when working collaboratively with their peers on group tasks.

Although this cannot happen overnight, once we have introduced and developed an awareness of the learning processes the next step is to provide the language with which to name and examine this process.

Phase 2: Immersion in the language

In our work in schools, we have found that metacognition and talking about learning comes more naturally when it is embedded in the daily life of the classroom. We need to use the language all the time, not just in specific metacognition lessons. As the learning is happening throughout a school day, the awareness and articulation of the learning process should also be present throughout the day.

First let us look at some of the ways in which this might be done.

- Displays:
    - words on the classroom walls
    - on the smartboard, etc.
    - using photo displays.
- Make the language explicit:
    - naming the kinds of learning happening.
- Think aloud: using 'think alouds' as we model and teach:
    - at the start and at the end of lesson i.e. in the plenary
    - when opportunities arise during the lesson i.e. 'think alouds'.
- Working documents (evidence):
    - individual learning journal/PLP
    - in the teachers' planning format.

> 'Some of the less able children can find it tricky (to talk about their learning) but by having the words on the board or on their desk, they have got something to use and they feel that they are still part of it.' (Teacher, Roslin Primary School)

These approaches are revisited from various different perspectives throughout the book.

Display

It helps to have a display of the language of learning. Of course, younger pupils might benefit from having more visual cues and reminders. For example, with emerging readers this vocabulary might be accompanied by photographs of the children engaged in such learning processes.

Case Study 2: Creating photo-cues

Pupils were asked to help to create photo-cues for different learning processes. They chose a pose or image to represent each process and they took the photographs themselves.

There was something significant about their involvement and ownership of this whole experience that deepened their understanding of the process and the language used to describe it. It was as if actually 'acting it out' helped them to visualise what each element of thinking and learning looks like and *felt like*.

> 'I think there is an impact on their understanding of what they are learning and why they are learning. They did the learning rounds recently and they were explaining we're not editing work because Miss Cameron told us to, we are editing it for a reason, and they then give those reasons, so I think there is an impact and on the confidence with what they are doing.' (Teacher, Roslin Primary School)

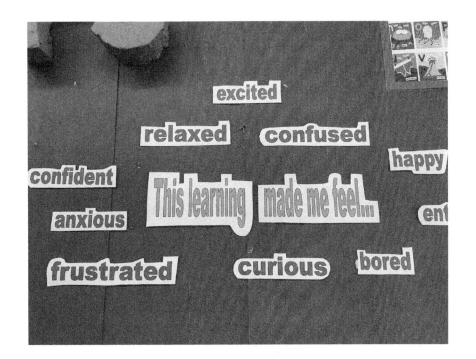

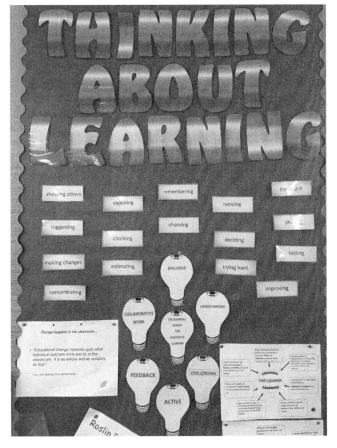

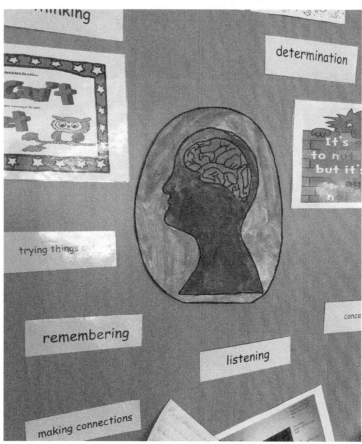

Make explicit

These displays can be referred to by pupils and teachers at any time. The language can be incorporated into a teacher's plan, and shared with the pupils alongside success criteria; better still, it should be simply embedded into the language of the classroom. For example, a teacher might, at the start of the lesson, make explicit what the pupils will be learning, and also how they will be developing their learning skills.

What we are learning:	'We are going to plan an investigation.'
How we are learning:	'We will be thinking, deciding and making suggestions.'
What we are learning:	'We are going to write a persuasive text.'
How we are learning:	'We are reading, thinking, using prior knowledge and skills; making decisions, trying out and redrafting.'
What we are learning:	'We are learning about how historians find out about the past.'
How we are learning:	'We will be using our senses to examine historical objects, thinking, using knowledge to make suggestions about the object.'

Think aloud

Using a think aloud approach enables the pupils to experience the process of thinking and learning. If the teacher verbalises the thought process this provides a model for pupils to follow. For example, when reading a short passage with a tricky word like 'onomatopoeia' the teacher might say something like:

Now this is a tricky word, I need to break it down.
'On', yes that bit is easy, 'on a mat', yes that's fine, 'on a mato' that's nearly it.
'Poeia', now that's really tricky, 'po-i-a', let's try that:
'on a matopoia', now that sounds familiar.
Where have I heard something like that? Ah yes, 'on a mat o pia'.
Does that sound right? Yes it does. 'on a mat o pia'.

So here the teacher is modelling a strategy, an approach that can be transferred to other situations. If pupils are familiar with such think alouds, and if they are encouraged to articulate their own think alouds, this makes a huge impact on their own metacognitive processes.

Another example in problem solving might be: How long is it until home time?

It is 2:40 now and we go home at 3:15.
From 2:40 until 3 o'clock is,
let's count in tens: 40–50–60 that's 20 minutes.
Now from 3 o'clock until 3:15 is 15 minutes.
I need to add the 20 minutes now to the 15, that means
20 add 10 add 5 which is 35 minutes.

> Now 35 minutes, does that seem about right?
> How did we solve the problem?
> We used our knowledge of how to count in tens, and our knowledge of time helped us to remember to stop at 60.

Most teachers would argue that they do the above. What are we doing that is different? In addition to making the problem-solving steps explicit, metacognition includes pulling together how we solved it. *We need to make explicit the learning processes, not just the steps to success.*

Involving the pupils in this articulation of the thought process helps to consolidate it in their minds. It lays down pathways that will eventually become familiar to them. For many learners this process provides the structure and framework, and indeed, the confidence to develop their own strategies. Many good maths teachers do this kind of thing intuitively. They do not just require an answer from the pupil, they seek an explanation of how they got there. It is strange that in maths, teachers have known for a long time that the journey is more important than the destination: the means of finding a solution is more important than the answer.

For metacognition we need to make this much more widespread across the curriculum. We need to teach about thinking and learning. We need transferable skills that will not become outdated. We need to encourage and nurture exploration of different ways of learning – but we cannot do this effectively if we do not develop the language with which to model and share it.

> 'I think it's been good exposing the children to more of the words, and the terminology that they use for learning has been useful. We displayed those next to the smartboard and we hand the words out at the beginning of each week so each child has a different learning word, so the more they see them they start using those words more often whereas before they hardly ever used them to be honest.' (Mr Swan, class teacher)

The language of learning can be incorporated into prompts, posters or resource sheets. These can be used to help focus a child's thinking about the way that they are learning at different points in a task. An example of this is discussed in more detail in Chapter 3.

Working documents

- Working documents (evidence):
  - individual learning or progress file
  - in the teachers' planning format.

In one nursery where we worked, the staff felt that they would include the relevant learning words in the label for certain photographs in the children's individual folders. For example where the child making a model said they *looked and copied* to help them make it, these words would go next to the photograph of the child and the model for the child to look at and talk about with nursery staff and parents.

The language of learning and how it is incorporated within daily life is actually more of an iterative process than a linear one. Such incorporation into plans, teaching and learning activities as described above is a way to immerse the children in the language, but it also relies on

understanding and increasing familiarity of metacognition, of thinking and talking about learning. Once the children have some experience of thinking about their learning and some vocabulary with which to articulate this, a more effective approach would be a metacognitive language cycle.

Phase 3: The metacognitive language cycle

At this point it is helpful to introduce the metacognitive language cycle. This provides an idea of the 'Model, Teach, Make explicit' approach to metacognition. Later in this book the information and examples provided will illustrate how the elements link together and give more detail of what each element means.

We have already discussed the value and different approaches to *modelling* the language and processes of learning. Teaching and reviewing will look different according to the phase in which you are placed. We will go into more depth on *teaching* and *reviewing* when discussing specific age groups in the later chapters.

Whatever the age we have as our focus, it is important to make metacognition explicit.

Making the metacognition explicit

Through heightened awareness, pupils will become used to considering how they learn. So how is making it explicit different? As an introduction to metacognition or the language of learning, it can be helpful to teach the class something completely new and different, unconnected to other work, so that the focus of the lesson becomes metacognition rather than something specific in maths or history.

MODEL
Teachers should use think
alouds to explicitly model
the thinking processes.

REVIEW
At the end of the lesson, or
the start of another one,
remind the pupils of the
kind of strategies they
have been/will be using.
Get them to consider/
reflect and share ideas
about 'ways of learning',
so they are aware of the
options for *learning best*.

ETHOS
Create a supportive
ethos where it can
be made explicit.

TEACH
Explicitly refer to the kind
of learning. (e.g. How do
we remember? We can use
a mindmap, notes, rhymes,
etc.) Demonstrate, model,
use think alouds. Develop a
range of approaches so the
pupils can select an
approach that best suits
their own learning style.

MAKE EXPLICIT
Talk about the strategies
used. Display the words
that describe the language
of learning. Find ways to
make visual the thinking
processes.

Figure 2.1 The metacognitive language cycle

For example the case study below uses a lesson on language to highlight some of the learning skills we use instinctively but with different degrees of confidence and competence.

Case Study 3: Counting in a foreign language

One way is to teach the class how to count in a lesser known foreign language. At the start of the lesson, no-one knows how to count in this language; at the end of a short lesson, the children are able to count.

What happened in between not knowing and then being able to count? A class discussion on what they did and how they learned can help pupils focus on the learning process:

we *listened, repeated, tried to remember, drew on what we knew* about counting and number in English to help us with order etc.

Such a discussion opens up opportunities for children to talk about the different ways in which they learn, in this case: *remembering*. For example, when we did this activity in French with an upper primary class some explained that they remembered because the sound of the words reminded them of something: children remembered *quatre-vingt* because it sounded like *catch a van*.

Some of the children talked about images that came to mind when they heard or said the word. Others were actively applying their knowledge of another language: e.g. *fyra* sounds like *four* so they remembered this connection. (*Fyra* means four in Swedish if you didn't know!)

In Case Study 3 above, the activity for teaching children to count was a fairly transmissive one: the teachers talk/gesticulate, the pupils listen. There might be some games, but the learning processes are dependent on listening and auditory/visual memory.

A follow-up lesson we might do with the intention of increasing further metacognitive awareness and language would be a more practical one. It would again involve teaching the class something they cannot already do: for example how to navigate a specific route, in a maze, on paper, in a computer game, etc., or how to make a model. The learning processes should be more practical: they could involve movement, spatial awareness, knowledge of directional language, the ability to interpret an instruction, amongst other processes. The key part of the lesson, however, will be the discussion at the end. Here we would focus upon *how* the children went from their inability to do the task to their relative success. The focus will be on the language necessary to articulate this. How did they learn? What were the processes involved? A comparison with the skills and processes involved in learning the language can enrich this discussion further.

It is essential that we involve the learners: as the pupils become more familiar with the language and the process of thinking about how they learn, they become more equal partners in being able to identify and articulate this together.

For example, being confident to hold up a card containing a word that describes the kind of learning that is actually happening during a class lesson if they notice that that is what they are doing (see Chapter 3).

As a teacher you need to focus on the *how* of learning by asking questions like: How did you do that? How do you know? And by being prepared to support the child to 'unpick' the how.

Consider the young child trying to make a tower. The tower gets too high and falls down. A learning conversation with the child can help them look at how they are building the tower, to notice the point at which it falls down and to think about why it falls down.

- Is there anything they can do differently?
- Are they likely to achieve success by trying the same approach over and over again?
- The child may then begin to see a way to strengthen the tower so that it can be higher. What did they learn that helped them to modify the tower?

Children can make these revisions without support, but a metacognitive learning conversation can help them be more aware of what they have done that was successful: to be conscious of the understandings that helped them to modify the tower.

This move from implicit to explicit can help embed the learning.

Creating an appropriate ethos

In order to create a supportive ethos where metacognition can be made explicit it is necessary to provide time where it can be acknowledged and discussed. It is important to plan to make metacognition explicit on a regular basis and to seize opportunities when children are overheard using the language of learning. Pupils also need to be supported in finding the appropriate words to articulate and name a process when talking about their learning. Effective articulation should be celebrated in the same way as any other successful learning in a classroom.

In addition to the ongoing focus on metacognition and the language of learning, opportunities for discussion need to be planned into the weekly timetable. This allows quality time for tasks that develop strategies and solutions, building transferable skills.

Think about it, talk about it, go away with a new set of skills to apply in the future. Having a dedicated time for these discussions indicates the value which we put upon this integral aspect of learning.

Individual learning or progress files

Learning journals and personal learning planning

In many schools nowadays pupils from a very young age are expected to talk and think about their learning. Schools often have a weekly session where pupils are encouraged to look back at their learning and to set themselves targets for the following week.

In our experience in looking at these plans we noticed that children can struggle to find meaningful words to describe what it is they wish to develop. If we do not teach the language and some knowledge of the ways we learn then it is always going to be difficult to articulate what we want to work on in order to learn *better*.

If, in the ways described earlier, we can make thinking and talking about how we learn more of a normal part of classroom practice then pupils will find it much easier to talk, write and plan to learn better.

Planning for learning about learning

A change in the way that teachers think about their own planning is required if we are to be successful in making metacognition more explicit in the classroom.

Teachers need to plan for the learning, as they normally would; however, they should also consider *the kind of learning* that is likely to take place. Being more aware of *how the children will learn*, as well as *what* they will learn will make it easier to develop this awareness in the pupils. It may be that an additional column would be added to forward plans so that there is somewhere to indicate the kind of learning to be focused upon. It may be that there is a section on the planning format where learning about learning might be addressed.

This is not to suggest that there needs to be unnecessary bureaucracy and paperwork, but that integrating learning about learning into the plans should be possible in a way that is beneficial and not too onerous.

Phase 4: Reflection

Of course developing a reflective ethos in class is very important and many of the suggestions in this book will enable the class teacher to get children talking about their learning. A more structured way of doing this is through peer learning interactions which will be discussed in Chapter 4.

You cannot establish a metacognitive approach without the language, but there is more to it than just the language. In the next chapter we will explore how to build on this language basis whilst taking part in reflection on the learning processes.

Summary and key points

In this chapter we have explored the language of learning and how to begin enabling pupils to start to be more aware of how they learn and their learning processes. We have considered ways to make these processes much more explicit. Below is a summary of the phases that we have explored in this chapter.

Phase 1: Heighten awareness

- talk about how we learn
- word banks displaying words that describe the learning processes.

Phase 2: Immersion in the language

- displays
- make explicit how we are learning
- think aloud
- working documents.

Phase 3: The metacognitive language cycle

- the cycle
- make explicit
- create the ethos
- individual learning
- planning for learning.

Phase 4: Reflection

- talking and thinking about how we learn.

Next steps for the reader

You might now wish to introduce some of these into your own school or classroom. It is important however that you do not go for a revolution where you attempt to do everything at once. It is much better to do something, little and often. The most important steps are

- use the language;
- make the learning processes explicit;
- have the learning conversation.

Reference

Mercer, N. (1995) *The Guided Construct of Knowledge*. Clevedon: Multilingual Matters.

3 Reflection and metacognition

This chapter focuses on how to model, encourage self-awareness of and articulate learning - the what, why and how of modelling the metacognition process. We will consider some of the different elements of metacognition. In particular we will discuss how we might develop the learner's own awareness about how they learn. This chapter builds on the work on developing language explored in Chapter 2 and explores a teacher's role in helping a child become more aware of how they learn. We suggest ways in which a teacher can use learning conversations in different curriculum areas and explore how to teach reflection. The chapter identifies and gives examples of a range of strategies and approaches that can be used to develop reflection and awareness of learning.

Introduction

- How can the teacher model and make explicit the process of learning?
- How can a teacher help a child to become aware of how they are learning?
- How can we support the child to articulate their reflections and encourage peer learning interactions?

This chapter illustrates how to model awareness of the learning process through think alouds and how to engage in learning conversations in order to make the learning more explicit. It has the following structure:

Modelling and making explicit the process of learning

1   Having the 'learning conversation' in different curricular areas:
   a)   Maths
   b)   Literacy
   c)   PE
   d)   Expressive arts

Helping the pupils to become aware of how they are learning

2   Explicitly teaching ways of reflecting:
   a)   Using the words
   b)   Profiling the words
   c)   Word displays
   d)   Identifying learning skills
   e)   Activities
        Using a learning carousel
        Making a poster
   f)   A process-aware approach
   g)   Learning monitors
   h)   Thinking about thinking and learning
   i)   Making *how* we learn part of classroom practice

If we want the learners in our care to learn better, we need first to develop their awareness of *how they learn*. This can be done in a number of different ways.

1 Having the learning conversation

a) Maths: multiplication

Having the learning conversation before:
This is where the teacher would talk explicitly about metacognition and how we learn. It might, for example, be a short session outlining the kind of thinking that goes with the following activity.

Teacher:	Today we are working on our times tables.
Pupil:	We need to be able to recall these very quickly.
Teacher:	What strategies do you know that are useful for remembering something?
Pupil:	You could say it over and over again.
Teacher:	What else might you do?
Pupil:	You might remember an answer close to the one you are after, and then do a sum.
Teacher:	Can you give us an example?
Pupil:	If you don't know 6 x 4 but you do know 5 x 4 = 20, you can do 20 + 4 = 24.
Teacher:	Excellent. You have *remembered other learning* and *used that learning* here.
Teacher:	Does anyone know any other strategies?

This investigation into *ways of remembering* might be done before the actual lesson begins. It would be beneficial and relevant for the work that follows. It would also be a transferable skill that the pupils might apply in other curricular areas where quick recall remembering is important.

Having the learning conversation during:

As the lesson progresses the teacher should take opportunities to keep an awareness of what we are doing and *how we are learning*. For example:

Teacher:	What is 7 x 8?
Pupil:	56.
Teacher:	Good, how did you *remember* that one?
Pupil:	Well I did 8 x 8 = 64 and then I took away 4 making 60 and then took away 4 to make 56.
Teacher:	Well done, that's an interesting method. Did anyone do it differently?

Having the learning conversation after:

At the end of the lesson some discussion about the learning skills should be had so that the pupils are aware of the transferable skills and where they might be applied in other contexts and other curricular areas.

Teacher:	Today we have been *thinking* and *remembering*. What other learning skills do you think we had to use?
Pupil:	Remembering.
Pupil:	Listening.
Pupil:	Working together.
Pupil:	Calculating.
Pupil:	Trying until you work it out.
Teacher:	Yes these are learning skills. Where else would you use these?
	Who can tell me subjects or situations where you have to listen and remember?
Pupil:	When we do our comprehension.
Pupil:	Using the computer to find information.
Pupil:	When we are talking about tactics for football training.
Teacher:	Yes. What about *working together* and *trying out*?

The learning conversation above illustrates how it is possible to conduct a typical lesson whilst introducing the language of learning. These words are necessary if we want pupils to understand *how* they learn.

This is all very well in maths, where such an approach to the different methods used by pupils to work out problems has been used so well in the past, but what about other areas of the curriculum?

b) Literacy: reading

Let us now look at another context for learning about how we learn: a literacy lesson when pupils are required to summarise the information from a text.

Having the learning conversation before:

Teacher:	So, when you are doing this task, what kind of learning are we doing? What skills will we need?
Pupil:	Reading and thinking. Reading for information, we need to be able to *read* the passage quickly and *sort out* the important details and be ready to *share* them in our own words.
Teacher:	Yes you will be *thinking*, *reading*, *sorting* and *sharing*. These are all important learning words.
	Let's now think about what we might do. Let's talk about *using a strategy*, which is another learning skill. What might you do to tackle this challenge? What ways do you know for this kind of activity?
Pupil:	Well I like to use a highlighter, and I colour in the bits that I think are important.
Teacher:	Any other strategies?
Pupil:	I like to look for key words and underline them first. Then I look back and see if I can put what I am noticing into my own sentences.

Having the learning conversation during:
The teacher can develop these suggestions and encourage the pupils to try each strategy before deciding if they find one of these easier than the approach they are accustomed to already.

Having the learning conversation after:
After doing this it is important to discuss, at some point, how this approach might help them in other areas of the curriculum, for example when reading instructions or a timetable it is sometimes useful to highlight or underline key words.

It might now be useful to begin a learning word bank on a display so that you, and the pupils, can refer to it as each learning skill comes up in lessons. See below for more on displays.

c) PE: gymnastics

In putting a gymnastic sequence together the teacher might ask that each of three movements be combined together. Initially the movements might be done separately.

Teacher:	Now that you each have three movements you need to plan how you might combine them together in a sequence. Talk to your learning partner and *discuss* how you *plan* to do this. *Explain* to them how you will do the transition from one movement to another. Tell them how you came to your *decision*. Try to *explain* your thinking.
Here the teacher is making explicit the learning words that describe how the children are learning.	

Putting emphasis on these words or referring to the words on a classroom display makes the learning process much more visible.

A possible response might be:

Pupil: I thought about the first one and the second one and tried to find something similar - like the way I held my arms out. I thought, yes that would be a good way to have a link from the first to the second. Then for the change from two to three I couldn't do the arms again so I thought I could just show a similar shape. So I just thought about how it would look and looked for patterns and similarities.

Teacher: Good - you have a *plan*; you *thought it through*; you *looked for a pattern*.

Now let's *practise* and then *review*, giving each other *feedback* to see if you need to *make any improvements*.

Of course you will not be spending a great amount of the activity time discussing these words. Simply using them and making them more visible at the time will be enough to raise their profile. In the lesson plenary, or later on in the classroom you might return to the lesson and ask the class which learning words and skills they remember using or hearing. This in turn will provide an opportunity to have a learning conversation about learning itself, and thinking about how we learn. This could then lead on to discussing how some of these skills might be used elsewhere in their learning, in or out of school.

The teacher might ask, 'Can you think of other work where a similar thinking is required, for example Art or Drama?'

d) Expressive arts: drama

In drama the focus might be on gesture and facial expression. The teacher might begin as usual with some discussion of the learning intention and success criteria, one of which might be the way we convey emotion using gesture and facial expression.

The teacher might ask:

Teacher: How will we know if we are conveying our feelings?
Pupil: Well the others in the group will see and be able to react.
Pupil: Or we could ask them to guess how we are feeling.

In order to link with our metacognitive thinking here it would be useful for the teacher to encourage the pupils to think about their collaborative group skills, or the peer learning skills such as providing constructive feedback.

Teacher: So when you are the audience what will you need to do?
Pupil: We will need to *watch* carefully and listen.
Pupil: We need to think about what they are doing and *decide* if it is working on us.

Teacher: And when you are giving feedback what will you need to do?
Pupil: We need to *describe* how we saw it and how it made us *react*.
Pupil: We need to tell them things they might do differently.
Pupil: We need to be careful to be positive and not upset them.
Teacher: When you have got the feedback what will you do next?
Pupil: We need to *consider* what they have told us.
Pupil: We need to *review* our performance and make it better.
Pupil: We need to try again to *improve* it.

Later in a plenary we might ask the class to consider the learning skills they were using during performing, observing, reviewing and improving. The teacher would need to scaffold the words to elicit the learning skills indicated above in italics.

2 Explicitly teaching ways of reflecting

Of course if we want our pupils to articulate this so eloquently we cannot leave this to chance. Elsewhere in this book we talk about using the language of learning to model such articulations.

a) Using the words

The teacher may demonstrate this peer feedback and use think alouds, for example saying:

As I watched you I was *assessing* how well you were using your body language to show how sad you were feeling.
I was *comparing* your facial expression to the person on the video and thinking how well you were doing it.
I was thinking of *constructive suggestions* about how you might *improve* the performance and *make it better*.

Using the words and making them more obvious is one approach. Another is to have the words there on a classroom display. As the class become more experienced in thinking about their learning new words can be added. However, there is little point in simply putting words on a display without first establishing what they mean.

b) Profiling learning words

It is useful to have a lesson focus on certain words in order to introduce the concept of the language of learning. A common word like *remembering* is worthy of some activities in order to arrive at a shared understanding of what the word means and how it applies to learning in all sorts of situations. For example:

Remembering

You might start with an activity that involves remembering: learning a new trick, a song, some facts or a series of numbers like tables. With younger learners it might mean simply playing Kim's Game.

A new song

For example in most schools the process for learning a new song follows this pattern:

1   Listen to the first line. Repeat it back.
2   Go over the next line. Repeat both.
3   Go over another line. Repeat all three.

When the activity is over ask the learners to reflect on what they have just been doing:

Teacher:	Think through what you just did. What did we do to help you to remember?
Pupil:	We had to listen and try the first line. Then when we went onto the second line we were practising the first one all over again.
Teacher:	Yes, you had to *listen*, and *try it out*. Then you repeated it and practised the whole thing.
	These words: *remember, listen, try out, practice,* are all words that describe how we learn.
	Can anyone tell me other times that you will need to use these learning skills?

Kim's Game

Look at the objects. Try to remember what is there. (The objects are covered up and one removed. The children are asked to remember what was there and is now missing.)

This time look at the objects and look for things that will help you to remember:

•   Are there any links? Do they have anything in common?
•   Are there objects that begin with the same initial?
•   Will that help you to remember them?
•   Try again.

Teacher:	Think about what we were just doing.
	Can anybody tell me how they went about remembering the things on the tray?
Pupil:	I just looked and … and remembered!
Teacher:	Think about how I asked you to look for connections between the things on the tray.
Pupil:	Well I looked for clues like all the things to do with pets … the dog and the bone and the lead … so when the bone was missing I knew.
Teacher:	Good! You *looked carefully* and you *thought* about connections.

You *linked* the things to do with pets and this helped you to *remember* the things on the tray.

Did anyone use a different *strategy for remembering*?

Pupil: Yes I looked for the things beginning with 'p' and 'b' and then when something was missing I thought of all of these words and decided that the 'b' was missing.

Teacher: That was a good idea. Let's all try a different strategy for *remembering* this time and we can see if there is one that works better for them.

The teacher might actually write these words up on the board or on a display so that the pupils have them visible.

On other occasions the class can be encouraged to spot the learning words that apply to a lesson that is in progress. Alternatively the teacher can finish a lesson by asking the class to spot the learning skills they have been using during a lesson.

The main point here is that the word '*remember*' is profiled. There is a shared understanding of what it means. Strategies for remembering are shared and explored. Pupils are invited to try different strategies in order to establish what works best for them in a given situation.

This is learning about learning, and each individual has the opportunity to find out ways of remembering that might work best for them.

Appendix 3 profiles other words with suggestions about how they might be explored in a lesson focusing on the language of learning.

c) Word displays

Having the words on display is an effective way of demonstrating that these words – and the skills that they represent – are valued and important for learning. The teacher can refer to them before, during or after each lesson.

The pupils too can be encouraged to refer to them if they see opportunities. However, the teacher will need some process or system for managing this so that it doesn't become disruptive or interfere with the general flow of learning in the classroom (see below).

d) Identifying the learning skills

In one school the pupils were given a sheet with a list of learning words on it. At the end of each lesson the children were asked to colour in any learning skills they thought they had been using (see Appendix 5.1). At the end of the week the class reviewed the learning across the week. They discussed the words that were coloured most often as well as those that often got missed out. Then the teacher got the class to help work on these skills so that they weren't missed.

e) Activities

Using a learning carousel

It may be that a class activity like a learning carousel is necessary (see Appendix 1.7).

Divide the class into six groups with poster paper at each group. Each poster has one of the following questions written in the centre (you could choose four or six questions from the following eight, depending on the age and experience of your class):

1   What is learning?
2   What learning do we know we do?
3   Where do we learn?
4   How do we learn?
5   How do we talk about learning?
6   How do we learn best?
7   How can our learning be transferred?
8   How can we help others to learn?

Each group has a pen and gets around 3–4 minutes to write down their ideas on the poster in response to the question.

After 4 minutes or so move each poster round to the next group and get them to look at the comments already listed. It is a good idea to give each group a different coloured pen (so you can see which ideas come from each group). You might also ask each group to read each comment and put a tick or cross to indicate whether or not they agree and a question mark if they don't understand the comment.

Next give them 3 or 4 minutes to add their own thoughts to the question.

Repeat this so that each group tackles at least three of the poster questions. Generally three is enough to generate enough data to work on before children lose interest or feel that everything they would have said has already been said.

For a carousel like this you might get responses such as those below:

Carousel question *1*: *What is learning?*
Possible responses:

*   gaining information
*   getting better at something
*   developing skills
*   improving on something you already know or can do.

Carousel question *2*: *What learning do we know we do?*
Possible responses:

*   how to: play games, do sport, participate in music, art, drama
*   how to: find out things, information, skills, how to do other things
*   about information: knowledge, facts, figures
*   attitudes: we learn about right and wrong and the right or appropriate things to do

- about our world: what works and doesn't about life and science and nature and animals
- about technology: about how to switch things on and off, how to work a number of gadgets, electronic aids and games.

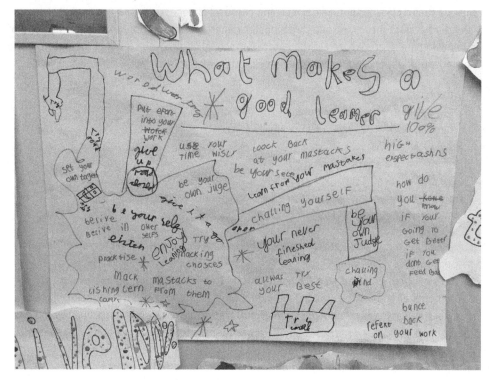

Carousel question 3: *Where do we learn?*
Possible responses:

- at school: in and out of classes, from our teachers, our peers and by ourselves
- at home: from our parents, friends, siblings, on our own
- everywhere: on the way to and from school, playing out, visiting people/places, on holiday, out shopping, etc.
- from: books, people, TV, the Internet.

Carousel question 4: *How do we learn?*
Possible responses:

- observing and copying
- doing what the teacher tells us
- exploring
- trying and experimenting
- remembering
- applying
- failing and trying again

- using skills or knowledge gained elsewhere in different situations
- problem solving
- communicating
- asking questions and clarifying
- trial and error
- following instructions
- persevering.

Continue as above for carousel questions 5, 6, 7 and 8.

It is clear that a carousel like this can get everybody thinking and talking about how they learn. It may be that you select only four questions for the carousel so that the pupils do not get carousel fatigue where they find there is nothing more to add to the posters. It may be useful to have two carousel sessions and divide the questions between them. Alternatively, group work might be done where each group has to discuss and provide a poster of their response to one of the questions.

How we learn better

Of course it is not enough to simply highlight what we mean by learning. The above carousel activity can provide a lot of information to explore in later sessions. For example, the responses to *'What is learning?'* might be explored so that all pupils have a shared understanding. Photographs might be taken of pupils doing these things; this, in turn, can be a useful resource and visual cue to remind them when they are using different learning approaches or aptitudes.

'What learning do we know we do?' is an attempt to reassure them that they are learning all of the time: whether it is watching TV or playing a computer game. The important point is that they have this cognition, this awareness that it all counts as learning as long as it is in some way transferable.

'Where do we learn?' might enable children to realise more fully that learning is how we live and should not be only associated with the more formal learning that takes place in school. It is particularly useful for pupils to realise that playing on a games console is still counted as learning. It is important that they understand that the input they bring to these situations, such as effort, concentration, perseverance, problem-solving skills and resilience is just as valid and vital when playing games on gadgets, playing sport, learning a musical instrument or learning new things in school.

This idea can be reinforced when looking at their responses to *'How do we learn?'*. *'How do we learn?'* should enable pupils to articulate what they already know about the language of learning. It is important to build upon what they know about how they learn so that it moves away from reflection into action. If you know that trial and error is one approach to use when solving problems, you need to explore how this approach can be improved. For example trial and error need not be a random scattergun approach. Pupils might feel able to experiment with more organised approaches such as organised lists or more systematic approaches to solving problems, whether in maths or other curricular areas.

The important thing is that we try to move from identifying how the children learn to how they might learn better another time. This element of the whole process is very important. Whatever stage of the school you are in, when discussing learning it is important to make the learning itself explicit. Next investigate *how* we learn, and then consider how we might *learn better* another time and in another situation:

1   Make the learning explicit.
2   Articulate what the learning is.
3   Explore how we learn this.
4   Consider how we learn this better another time.
5   Look for opportunities to transfer this learning.
6   Plan how you might learn better next time.

Making a poster

If, for example, you are doing some work where gathering and displaying information is required you might get the pupils to record their learning on a poster. This might be done individually or in small groups. Such an activity enables many different learning elements to be explored and developed.

Metacognition for making a poster
In order to create an effective poster pupils have to be able to

- *find information*;
- *organise* it;
- *articulate* what they feel is the most relevant information to convey;
- *select* the appropriate words and images to do this;
- *decide* how to *structure* this on the page;
- *communicate/share/negotiate* with others in order to get their own ideas down;
- keep to the allocated time and resources;
- *review and present* their work at the end.

With all of this going on it would be easy to swamp pupils with metacognition!

However it might be worth getting them to at least identify and list some of these skills initially. Later on, when the class are more familiar with the language of learning and are able to identify some of this learning for themselves, it is important to have more of a focus.

f) A process-aware approach

Identify the learning

The most important thing is that a little time is spent on identifying the learning processes during each lesson. The teacher might need to draw the pupils' attention to one or two of the learning elements during or after the lesson and get the pupils to work in pairs, discussing how well they felt they managed.

Review one or two elements of the learning

For example, following a language lesson where they had to organise and present information and to structure their ideas and images on the page they might reflect that:

'The layout was rushed or could have been better organised.'

Next they need to *consider next steps for improvement another time*. This might lead to a discussion about how they might learn better another time. The conclusion might be:

'We should have arranged everything on the poster first before we stuck it down.'

In order for this conversation to enable everyone to think and talk about learning beyond this particular example it is important to guide the discussion to what we can learn to use another time.

Think about transferable learning

This is where pupils should think about other activities or work where they might transfer this learning. For example, when making a leaflet, newspaper page or a collage, or when involved in a craft activity, they should remember to think about the layout and not to stick everything down until they are happy with it. Or they may realise that the process of reviewing and working out how to improve their work could be transferred to other tasks such as story writing.

g) Learning monitors

In one class we visited the teacher had two monitors for each lesson whose job it was to help everyone to realise when certain skills were being used. During the lesson these two monitors were allowed to hold up a card if they saw one of the focus words in action.

For example, during an imaginative writing lesson the teacher explained that she was looking for children who could

- share creative ideas;
- justify their opinions;
- suggest powerful vocabulary.

As the lesson progressed the learning monitors were allowed to hold up the special LM card (learning monitor) to attract the teacher's attention. (Example cards can be found in Appendix 6.2.)

This meant that the lesson was not disrupted but that the teacher could choose to stop and take the opportunity to explore some of the language of learning at an opportune time. It also meant that the learning monitors, or 'meta-monitors', themselves had to be able, not only to spot the learning, but to be able to share and justify what they meant too.

h) Thinking about thinking and learning (see Appendix 1)

Appendix 1.6 provides an example of an approach that might be used to get the pupils thinking about the language of learning in a reflective manner. They are given a sheet with some of the language of learning words on it. They are asked to think back over the day or week and try to settle on some of their learning that was memorable for them in some way. The intention here is that we give them ownership of their reflection about learning. They should have the choice to talk about something that meant something to them; something they are pleased with or perhaps something they struggled with. On occasions it might be that the teacher would find it more beneficial to direct the class to reflect on the same lesson so that they can draw new learning out of the result of this activity.

The pupils are asked to colour in two words from each section. They are asked to consider words that applied at the start, during and at the end of their learning. The aim is that they are encouraged to think about the lesson in terms of the learning and of the learning skills. Reading the words and deciding on which apply enables them to focus on *how* they learned. Of course this will make more sense to them if they have already done some of the activities above that help the class to gain a shared understanding about what the words actually mean!

i) Making how we learn part of classroom practice

One way to highlight learning in the classroom is to make a space for it in your timetable. It would be very easy to start with a passion and have a few one-off lessons on learning and then fall back into old ways. Whereas if you were to make a space in the timetable where there is a commitment to talk about learning every week you will be more likely to maintain some kind of dialogue about learning in your classroom.

Having a regular slot means of course needing some kind of structure for the session. It may be that in such a space there is a whole class focus. You might, for example, focus on one learning word each week: for example, *deciding*. A shared understanding would be explored with the class. You might take a key question approach like this:

*   What do we mean by deciding?
*   What kind of things do we need to decide?
*   What strategies do you use to decide?
*   What do you do if you can't decide or can't agree with your group about a decision that needs to be made?
*   How can we get better at deciding?

(See Appendix 3.1 for other ideas about deciding.)

If such a focus is taken over a number of sessions, then the class will be more aware of some of the components of learning and be better able to articulate their own capacities.

The above approach could also be employed as a topic for assembly where the whole school is asked to focus on one element of learning and then spend some time in class as a follow up, exploring what this word means to them (see Appendix 3). We should not take it for granted that children know what we mean by words like remembering, deciding, etc. They may not even have a shared understanding of what we mean by learning itself.

Process for planning

The above examples could provide a working frame for raising awareness of metacognition in the classroom on a regular basis:

*   Identify the learning.
*   Make how we learn explicit.
*   Identify one or two things to develop.
*   Consider next steps for improvement.
*   Identify transferable learning.

In the next chapter we will explore some ideas about how we might support and develop pupils' ability to articulate their thinking about their own thinking and learning.

Summary and key points

In this chapter we have considered some ways to model and make explicit the process of learning. We have explored some ways in which a teacher can use learning conversations in different curriculum areas and how to teach children to reflect. We have explored ways to support the child to articulate their reflections and encourage peer learning interactions, and we have explored ways of making *how we learn* part of everyday classroom practice.

Next steps for the reader

Think about how you might employ some of the ideas from this chapter in your day-to-day practice. You might take two approaches to this, one on *planning* and the other on *reflecting*.

Process for planning:

- Identify the learning.
- Make how we learn explicit.
- Identify one or two things to develop.
- Consider next steps for improvement.
- Identify transferable learning.

Process for reflecting:

- Identify the learning.
- Review one or two elements of the learning.
- Consider next steps for improvement another time.
- Think about transferable learning.

4 Developing metacognitive processes

In this chapter we will explore some ideas about how to support and develop pupils in their ability to articulate their thinking about their own thinking and learning. The focus will be on the kind of dialogue that can be facilitated in a classroom: between teacher and pupils, pupils and their peers, and in monologues through the 'peer learning interactions'. The chapter explores how to maximise the opportunities in a school day to make explicit the learning processes and immerse children in the language of learning. Practical examples are included to illustrate how some of the strategies might be achieved.

Introduction

Learning conversations help us to articulate what we know about how we learn. This chapter explores the benefits of learning conversations through the following headings:

1   Looking for opportunities
2   Structuring the reflections
    a)   Using pro formas
    b)   Learning monitors
    c)   Using a card sort
    d)   Post-its
3   Sharing the reflections
    a)   Personal learning planning
    b)   Wall displays
    c)   Peer learning interactions
4   Learning
    a)   Learning councils
    b)   Having a focus on learning
    c)   Learning pit stops
5   Generally responding to opportunities

In Chapter 3 we considered the benefits of raising an awareness of metacognition. Having the learning conversation and doing things like using think alouds to articulate how we learn is an important element in enabling learners to acquire the vocabulary for discussing their own learning. Making this discussion about how we learn a regular part of classroom discourse will enable learners to begin to consider their own learning style and to think about how they learn *best*.

1 Looking for opportunities

In a typical primary school there is so much to get through in a day. Nevertheless there are still opportunities to get everyone talking explicitly about how they learn. The important thing is trying to have the learning conversations little and often. We should be looking for opportunities

- at the start of each day;
- at the start of each lesson;
- at the end of each lesson/day;
- in a timetabled slot;
- through having incidental conversations.

Below we will look at each of these in a little more detail.

At the start of each day

It might be that each day begins with a summary of the recent learning. Many schools begin with such a recap accompanied by a focus on the learning intentions for the day. Such an approach may be enhanced simply by adding something about the skills that will be required. However, rather than adding a long list of skills to be developed, it might be better to have a focus on two or three. For example:

> This morning we will be working on 3D shape in our maths and continuing with our work on The Vikings with our research and recording in our factfiles. This afternoon we will be in the gym developing our balance sequences before we begin a new art topic where we will be exploring shape patterns.
>
> The learning skills I want us to focus on will be *looking for patterns* and *expressing our ideas*. Can anyone suggest where we might get to look for a pattern today? What about expressing ideas - what does that mean? What would it look like?

The above approach would set up the day with the class having a clear idea of the learning strategies/skills that are going to be developed. This approach can be linked to some of the suggestions elsewhere in this book where there are ideas about ways of making such discussions more visible.

At the start of each lesson

Something similar could be done at the start of a lesson, but not every lesson. It is important not to over-use the discussion, otherwise the pupils may well tune out. It would be better to select only one or two lessons per day in which to spend a little time discussing the focus learning skill. It is important that the discussion does not distract from the rest of the infor-mation required for the lesson. A good example might be the following:

Learning intention:

We are learning about the features of an effective leaflet.

   Success criteria:

- I can identify some of the features of a leaflet.
- I can use some of these features effectively in my own leaflet.
- I can provide feedback on what makes an effective leaflet.

Learning skills:

- *looking for evidence*
- *identifying* features
- providing effective feedback (*expressing and justifying thoughts and opinions*).

The above format could easily be the structure for lesson openings. Some time might be spent on the learning intentions so that the pupils know what they are learning. The success criteria will enable them to know what success will look like. The learning skills will help them to know *how* they are learning. Of course, the actual context for learning and the activities that the pupils will do would need to follow on from this introduction.

It is also useful at some point to help them to make the link to other learning by asking:

- Where else have you used these skills?
- Where else might it be useful?
- Think about in school and also beyond school, when you are out playing or shopping, for example.

At the end of each lesson/day

It will be useful to end the lesson with some link back to what you set out to do. This usually takes the form of a recap or plenary. It often involves the product of their labour: looking at a model that has been made, reading aloud a story that has been written, watching a play that has been created, etc. This kind of ending to the lesson provides an excellent opportunity to ask questions like:

- What have you learned?
- How have you learned?
- What transferable skills have you been using?

The important thing here is not that you take lots of time discussing the learning in depth, but instead, that you refer to it little and often, like many layers of varnish over time building up a glossy sheen.

It may be that there is not time to do this after every lesson. Therefore, it might be better to set aside 10 minutes at the end of the day to ask the class questions like:

- What have you learned?
- How have you learned?
- What transferable skills have you been using?

Better still, you might ask the questions and have the pupils work in twos or threes discussing their own responses. In this way they are all involved and all have the opportunity to explore how they have been learning throughout the day.

In a timetabled slot

The above ideas for the end of the lesson or end of the day may well be considered too time consuming in a busy timetable. Many schools have a timetabled slot set aside for learning conversations. Often such conversations lead into children writing something in their own learning journals or personal learning planning books. The suggestions above might well enable such discussions to be much more meaningful in terms of having an understanding of how we learn best.

Reserving a part of the week so that such conversations actually do take place is a good first step. However, it is possible that real reflection is seen as a once-a-week thing and not part of everyday learning. It would be important for the teacher to make sure that the children see the timetabled slot as something linked to all of their learning all of the time if it is to be of any use at all. It is crucial that the reflection on learning is meaningful and valued, and that it is not a token gesture or tick box activity.

2 Structuring the reflections

It might be beneficial to have some way of structuring these important learning conversations. It might be that you need to gather information to share with the class, the rest of the school, with parents or beyond the school community. You may wish to have reminders for the pupils in class, or you might want to have some record of the pupils' growing awareness of how they learn. (See Appendix 1.6; Appendix 1.2 could also be used.) Some ideas for structuring these learning conversations follow.

a) Using pro formas

(See Appendix 1.6; Appendix 1.2 could also be used.)

Having some sort of short list of words to describe the learning processes is a useful resource to share with the class. Ideally you will have already devoted some time to exploring what these words mean, either in your own class or in assembly (see Chapter 9). Providing the pupils with the list gives the opportunity to keep some tally of the kind of processes being used in each lesson. Pupils can colour in words that apply to each of the focus lessons over the course of a week. It is suggested that this is only used for focus lessons because it might be overkill to do this for every single lesson. Such a list serves both to remind pupils of how they might be learning as well as providing a record of the skills that are being used often or never. If skills are rarely used but still considered important, this assessment can inform next steps for planning teaching and learning activities aimed at exploring these skills.

b) Learning monitors

It might be beneficial to have one or two pupils whose task it is to monitor some of the learning skills and strategies covered over the course of the lesson/day. They might record and present this information during a plenary or reflective pit stop. This would give them the responsibility for thinking and reflecting on how the learning is achieved. It may be a child from the pupil council or learning council who is given this responsibility or it may be that this responsibility could be shared over time by everyone in class.

c) Using a card sort

(This activity and resources were first printed in Tarrant, P. (2013) *Reflective Practice and Professional Development* (London: SAGE) and are reproduced with permission from SAGE Publications.)

Appendices 1.4 and 1.5 provide the cards for this card sort activity, and Appendix 4.2 includes a set of instructions. Basically the idea is that the cards can be used by pupils to structure their reflections on their learning.

First of all the child will select a card that describes the activity that they wish to reflect upon. Next they take a card that describes how they think they approached the task, at the beginning, the middle, and end of the activity. They go on to select cards that describe how they felt about the learning and how well they feel they performed.

The point is for the children to become familiar with reflecting on the lesson and with the language of learning to articulate their reflections.

d) *Post-its*

Post-its can be used in a variety of ways. Pupils can have a set of blank Post-its on their tables and as a lesson progresses they can write any of the learning words they encounter on different Post-its. It may be that such an activity has to be introduced in a gradual and structured way. For example the teacher might suggest learning skills required for the task ahead, or they might ask the pupils to think of four learning skills that they might need for the task. Then as the lesson progresses there might be *reflective pit stops* (see below), during which the children have 5 minutes to think, talk and share their reflections on their learning so far. The teacher might ask:

* How are we learning so far?
* Talk to your learning partner and discuss which skills you have been using. Add any Post-its, if necessary.
* Are there skills that you thought you might use that haven't been needed? Why is that?
* Find out if your partner has faced any challenges or difficulties.
* Ask them how they might get on better for the next part of the lesson.

At the end of the lesson the teacher can ask each group to discuss the Post-its assembled before doing a sweep to share this learning. In doing so it will be useful not only to identify the words that describe how they have been learning (such as remembering, making connections, etc.) but to be able to say exactly when that skill was necessary. This could be developed into a conversation about which of these words and skills they found easiest or hardest and how they might be able to become *better* at it. For example:

* If you found remembering hardest, how can you improve at this?
* Can someone who found remembering easy in this lesson help those who found it hard?
* Who has strategies that they might share?

Teacher:	So, you have been writing words on the Post-its as we have gone through today's lesson. You will now have 5 minutes to share and discuss the words and how well you think you were with these learning skills.
Teacher:	Now the blue group, can you tell me two of your words and where in the lesson they occurred?

Pupil:	We have been *remembering* and *making connections*. We had to remember how to set out our report. We made connections to when we were doing this for the school open day only this time we had to imagine we were the Romans reporting on the big battle.
Teacher:	Okay, so who found remembering easy? Who found it hard? What about making connections? Can someone who found making connections easy help the others by explaining what they did and how they did it?

The above example enables pupils to have a meaningful and authentic discussion about how they learn. Such a discussion might well lead to exploring different approaches and strategies for learning. The Post-its can be put on a wall display as both a reminder of this learning and also as evidence of the ongoing process.

Another Post-it idea is simply to have a wall display with one or two words profiled each day. At the end of each lesson pupils can add Post-its to the display illustrating what they did in terms of the focus words, or they could add words of their own to the display. By the end of the day there would be sufficient data for a meaningful and authentic learning conversation about the language of learning and how we learn. As above, pupils could be asked to share how they go about these skills, as a way of helping others to become better at their learning.

3 Sharing the reflections

a) Personal learning planning

Many schools have adopted an approach towards their learning that involves pupils keeping a personal learning planning document. The basic idea is that pupils look at their work at the end of each week and write down something about their successes and then go on to set learning targets for the following week. Whilst this approach has many potential benefits for the pupils in terms of taking responsibility for their own learning, it also throws up many challenges. How do the children know what to write? Do they write what they need to or simply write something for the benefit of the teacher? How can they write something meaningful if they do not have the language of learning vocabulary?

Therefore, having the kind of experiences outlined in this book and a focus on this language of learning might be part of the solution to these challenges. If the children have had some of this language modelled, explored and discussed, they will be much better equipped for recording how they learn and how they might work on learning better in future.

b) Wall displays

Wall displays are a good way of having a focus on particular learning words or skills. It also provides a teaching opportunity (as discussed above). These displays can be in a classroom or can be part of a whole school initiative that shares this approach with the whole school community. Having displays in the corridors is a very good way of sharing this with parents and other visitors to the school so that the general message can be supported and reinforced.

Below you will see some examples of class and whole school displays. What they have in common is that they feature the language of learning and that they are organic as opposed to finished displays. It is very important that such displays belong to the learners themselves. Opportunities for the pupils to engage with the display will make the display much more effective and meaningful in the long run. (See above for other ideas as to how to do this.)

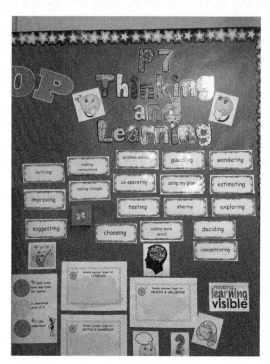

c) Peer learning interactions

A different approach towards articulating what we know about how we learn is to have a peer learning interaction (Tarrant 2013). A peer learning interaction is different from a learning conversation in that it doesn't really involve a two-way conversation. The point is that we tend to remember best the things that we had to work out for ourselves.

For a peer learning interaction to be successful it requires one person to ask the right sort of questions and be able to resist joining in or offering answers and advice. In my book *Reflective Practice and Professional Development* (Tarrant 2013), I offer some detailed ideas about how to set this up in the classroom.

Basically, one person has the responsibility of facilitating the thinking of the other person in the interaction. For clarity we call the person facilitating, 'the Listener', and the person thinking and talking about their learning, 'the Speaker'. The pupils need to explore what makes a good interviewer. They consider the kind of questions to ask, the right body language to adopt and the way to respond so that their peer learning partner does most of the talking. Having done all of this preparation, they might then take an opportunity to hold a peer learning interaction with a focus on *how* we learn. An example follows.

Listener:	Think of a lesson you have had this week that sticks in your mind for some reason.
Speaker:	Okay, I will choose the drama lesson we did yesterday.
Listener:	Why did you choose this lesson?
Speaker:	Because beforehand I didn't want to do the activity, and then I did it and now I am glad that I did!
Listener:	Can you tell me something about what you learned?
Speaker:	Well I learned that sometimes you just have to have a go, even when you don't really want to. If you don't try you don't learn, do you?
Listener:	Can you list some of the learning skills you might have learned in this lesson?
Speaker:	Well I had to *listen*, and to *try hard*, I had to *cooperate* and I had to *negotiate* my ideas – that was the bit I found hard. Nobody would listen to me at first.
Listener:	Tell me more about what you found hard?
Speaker:	....
Listener:	What did you have to do to get them to listen to you?
Speaker:	....
Listener:	Do you think that some of your learning skills improved in this lesson? If so, which ones and how did they improve?
Speaker:	....
Listener:	Where else in your learning might you use these skills?
Speaker:	....
Listener:	What might you do another time to make these skills even better?
Speaker:	....

As you can see from the above, the interviewer is not required to have a conversation. They are not there to share experiences or offer advice. Their job is to ask the questions.

Children require training and support to do this well. A question bank is useful for this (see Appendices 2.2, 2.3 and 2.4).

Facilitating peer learning interactions

In Appendix 2.1 you will find some suggestions for developing some of the interview skills required in order to facilitate pupils' talk about their learning. This process will take a number of sessions before each child is confident in their listening and questioning. They also need time to be able to 'step back' and allow the person reflecting to do most of the talking. However, it is well worth the investment if the end result is children who can take on the role of asking and listening or of reflecting on and articulating how they learn. You will also find some question starters in Appendix 2.1.

At the end of the interaction the pupils might record something about the conversation on a pre-prepared pro forma or writing frame (Tarrant 2013), or they might share one thing that they learned about their own learning somewhere on a wall display. It could even be noted in a Personal Learning Plan, but it is most important that the talking exercise does not turn into a writing exercise!

4 Learning

a) Learning councils

The school might have pupils who represent each class in a weekly gathering as a learning council. Part of their remit might be to share, develop and promote the language of learning. Their responsibility might be to help keep visible the way that the class are learning. This might involve contributions during lessons or the plenary at the end of lessons, or in other ways that remind us about the skills and strategies that contribute towards how we learn.

b) Having a focus on learning

Below is a focused session on learning. This example has maths as a focus but it could easily be adapted for any curricular area as it is the learning skills that are the focus and not the curricular outcomes.

Pupils arranged in groups are first asked to think about maths as a subject:

- When you think of maths what comes to mind?
- Does maths come in different headings?

It is likely the children will offer categories like:

shape, measure, number, problem solving, etc.

Each group is then given one of these as their context for discussing learning skills. The children are now asked to think of their category and mindmap all of the learning words that might be developed through related activities. For example, the group discussing measure might come up with:

thinking, sharing, estimating, guessing, taking care, recording.

At this point you might need to add some of the learning skills cards (Appendix 3) or refer to words on classroom displays in order to add to the learning words that each group come up with.

The important thing is that the children are thinking about how they learn in a specific subject or area of their classroom learning. The mindmap of words might be utilised later on in a classroom display that will remind the learners of how they are learning. It might also be necessary to select some of these words and unpack what they mean in the maths context.

At some point each group will share their words and the sum of their discussions. This activity should alert all of the children to the transferable nature of this learning. The teacher can draw out how looking for a pattern in shape also refers to number work and problem solving, for example.

This transferable nature of learning skills can be further highlighted with the next activity where the children are asked to select four or five of their words and think of situations beyond maths where they use these skills.

- Where else *in* school do we use these skills?
- Where *outside* of school do you use this skill?
- Can you think of examples of success in using this skill in and out of school?

The point here is to help children to realise that learning skills are useful for all sorts of learning in all subjects and contexts, whether it is how to solve a puzzle in maths, how to find the treasure in a computer game or how to bowl a ball that gets a someone out in cricket.

The above activities might be followed up with some discussion about how this understanding about how we learn in maths can be made more visible: classroom displays, assemblies, sharing of learning, posters, etc. Such an initiative can help to make thinking about how we learn much more part of the whole school ethos. (An outline plan for a session like this, with a focus on numeracy, can be found in Appendix 4.3.) Chapter 9 includes a version of this example in which we discuss a whole school approach to using a pupil learning council to spread the word.

c) Learning pit stops

It may be that in class you might introduce some sort of learning pit stop where an opportunity is taken to pause from working to make explicit the way pupils are learning. Pit stops can allow the teacher to use the language of learning and to tease out how they are learning. Or it could be an opportunity to ask pupils to try to identify which transferable learning skills they are using. The children could also be asked to share strategies they have been using so that others can 'try it their way'. Developing this 'sharing, experimenting and finding what works best for you' is an important learning skill in itself.

For a pit stop to be an effective teaching strategy it needs to be used sparingly. Like in the Grand Prix, there should be few pit stops and the skilled teacher will need to make sure that when they stop, they make it count!

5 Generally responding to opportunities

While the formal opportunities discussed above will be very beneficial and will give reflections about how we learn their rightful significance in a busy school week, it is also important to take other opportunities to have learning conversations. As detailed elsewhere in this book, it is essential that teachers use and reinforce the language of learning as often as possible. It is important to take opportunities to highlight and profile words that describe how we learn. It is important to explore some of these words so that a shared understanding exists in the minds of the teachers and the learners. Whole school approaches work best for this and some ideas about how to develop these will be discussed in Chapter 9.

Summary and key points

In this chapter we have focused on talking about how we learn in order to work out how we *learn best*. We have explored some ideas about how we might support and develop pupils in their ability to articulate their thinking about their own thinking and learning. We looked at different opportunities for talking about how we learn, such as learning conversations using pro formas and learning monitors. We explored some ways of sharing these reflections such as personal learning planning documents, wall displays and reflective learning pit stops. Above all, we have examined ways to support a classroom ethos where reflecting and talking about *how* we learn is part of our daily practice.

Next steps for the reader

Try to set aside 10 minutes at the end of the day to ask the class questions like:

- What have you learned?
- How have you learned?
- What transferable skills have you been using?

Better still, try to ask the questions and have the pupils work in twos or threes discussing their own responses. In this way they are all involved and all have the opportunity to explore how they have been learning throughout the day.

Look for other opportunities to try some of the approaches listed above.

Reference

Tarrant, P. (2013) *Reflective Practice and Professional Development*. London: SAGE.

5 Foundations for metacognition

This chapter discusses ways to build the foundation for a metacognitive approach to learning. While it is written with a focus on learning in a child-centred, play-based environment such as the nursery, it is useful reading for any teacher beginning a metacognitive approach in their classroom. There is consideration of the learning environment and the role of the adults in facilitating learning conversations and promoting thinking about learning. It identifies target language for this age group and explores ways in which an early years practitioner might incorporate this language of learning into existing routines. Through use of case studies and example interactions, it demonstrates ways in which the nursery practitioner might begin to make children more aware of how they are learning.

Introduction

Over the course of our research into developing metacognitive awareness for pupils in schools we have noted that a typical reaction in the initial stages of the programme is that metacognition 'just cannot be possible with the under-fives'. However, in most cases the introduction of a metacognitive approach is not very far removed from existing nursery practice. Most nursery practitioners already have a focus on building a child's vocabulary and on providing opportunities for the development of specific learning skills. In order to lay the foundations for metacognitive practice further up the school, often very few major changes need to be made. What is most necessary is that nursery practitioners, be they teachers, nursery nurses or learning assistants, feel confident about how what they are doing is supporting metacognition.

In this chapter we will explain how metacognition can be embedded into the nursery experience through considering the environment and the regular routines and practices of the setting. There is an expectation that the nursery will have opportunities for structured play with target learning intentions but that it will be predominantly child-led. Those working in a more structured nursery might find Chapter 6, which focuses on the early years, equally relevant to their practice.

Compared to other classrooms, the process for introducing metacognition is slightly different in the nursery, particularly when working in a child-led context. For this reason, we recommend reading some of the other chapters, such as Chapters 6–8, before returning to consider metacognition in the nursery. It is also useful for nursery staff to see how the work on metacognition in the early years is built on as the child progresses through the school.

Structuring the metacognition

Although learning in the nursery will have many elements that are child-led, there still needs to be a structure to the metacognitive approach. In the same way that nursery teachers have themes and learning outcomes for blocks of time, there also needs to be a loose plan for the integration of metacognition. It is helpful to identify a few metacognitive skills at a time on which to focus. These might be specific to the child or there might be a whole group focus. An aim for the end of the nursery stage might be for children to recognise when they are using the skills specified below and to be able to name them.

looking	listening	feeling
trying out/finding out	choosing/deciding	using imagination
thinking	remembering	sharing
taking turns	wondering	keep trying

A nursery setting brings its differences but metacognition remains the same. Taking a metacognitive approach in the nursery is about raising the children's awareness of *how they are learning* and giving them the language with which to describe this. Young children learn instinctively. It is highly likely that the children are not always aware that they are learning. They will be making a model, listening to a story, playing in the water or sand or chasing each other around on trikes, for example. What the nursery practitioner should aim to do is to help children gradually become more aware of how they are managing to make the model, follow the story or move around after their friends on the trike. Such awareness can deepen a child's learning and can be applied by the child when solving problems or having difficulties with what they are doing. It is far easier to find another way to achieve a task if we are aware of how we set about it in the first place.

It is clear that some activities lend themselves to dialogue better than others. The children chasing round on trikes might be better able to talk about the experience afterwards rather than while on their trikes, whereas the children in the sand might quite naturally begin to voice their thoughts as they play. It could be quite easy for the nursery practitioner to encourage a child to explain why they are doing what they are doing in the sand and whether they have found anything out. Exploratory talk, usually encouraged in the nursery, is the voicing of thought processes as a child works something out or consolidates half-formed hypotheses. In other words, they are talking about the thinking behind a task as they learn. The outcome or conclusion of exploratory talk is often the greater understanding of a concept or skill, but by bringing a metacognitive approach, the nursery practitioner may also encourage the child to notice and remember how the learning came about.

Case Study 1: Exploratory talk – seizing the opportunities for a learning conversation: playing with toy cars

A child is trying to play with small toy cars in an area of the nursery. There is a carpet mat which is decorated with a design of a town's roads.

> *I'm gonna go really really fast.*
>
> *Brrrrrmmmmmmm*
>
> Child pushes the car on the mat road, lets go, and the car continues only for a short while.
>
> *No. I want to go fast. Don't stop.*
>
> The child tries again. The car falters again after only a short while.
>
> *It needs a bigger push. I'm going to give it a bigger push. Come on, car!*
>
> The child pushes harder but the car soon loses its momentum on the carpet-like surface.
>
> *Stupid car! Come on!*
>
> *A really hard push. Go!*
>
> The car bounces off the mat onto the hard floor of the nursery where it lands and skids across.
>
> *Yeah! I did a trick.*
>
> *Speedy driver, not on the road, going to go fast, fast, fast!*
>
> The child pushes the car again on the nursery floor and it goes a greater distance.
>
> *My car goes better on the floor. It doesn't like driving on the road.*
>
> *Miss, Miss, look how fast my car goes...*

Teaching point

There are plenty of learning opportunities to take advantage of here. The child has invited the adult to get involved. The practitioner may choose to explore the difference between far and fast but, for the purposes of metacognition, in this example the adult is exploring what the child found out and how.

> Practitioner: Show me your car driving then, Sam.
>
> Child: Look. Brrmmmmmm. Look at me go! (The child puts the car on the hard nursery floor and pushes. The car travels quite a distance with some speed.)
>
> Practitioner: Wow! That was good. Why isn't your car on the road?
>
> Child: It doesn't work on the road. Look. Silly car stops. (The child demonstrates.) Now it goes a long way fast. (The child pushes the car on the floor and lets go.)
>
> Practitioner: I wonder why?
>
> Child: It doesn't like roads.
>
> Practitioner: Why doesn't it like the road?
>
> Child: Cause it can't go fast on the road. It just stops.
>
> Practitioner: Can you think why it stops?
>
> Child: Yes.

Practitioner:	Why do you think it stops?
Child:	It doesn't like the road.
Practitioner:	Let's think why. How can we find out?
Child:	I don't know.
Practitioner:	Look carefully at the road and the floor.
Child:	The road is bumpy and the floor is smooth and slidey. Feel it with your hands.
Practitioner:	So it is. So why do you think the car goes better on the floor?
Child:	It likes slidey bits. The wheels work better on slidey bits.
Practitioner:	Shall we try again on another slidey surface?
Child:	I could drive it on the table.
Practitioner:	Go on then. See if it works on the table. (The child does.)
Practitioner:	Well done. What have you found out?
Child:	My car likes slidey things to drive on.
Practitioner:	How did you find out?
Child:	It went better on the slidey things. Look!
Practitioner:	That's right. You *found out* by *looking* and *touching* carefully and by *trying out* different places to drive your car. Well done!

Analysis of interaction

It is quite likely that the child has moved away to continue playing with their car in other places by this point, but it is important to begin to introduce the language of learning and to get the child to begin to think of how they achieved something. In order to sustain a conversation of this length we need the child's interest and focus to remain on the activity for the duration. As early years practitioners will be aware, this is not always possible. But in this example, the child, keen to share their discovery initiates conversation with the adult, signalling a willingness to talk. The child is obviously very interested in what they are doing. Both these aspects make this a favourable time for a learning conversation. The learning conversation or processes discussed can be revisited at other times or recorded. For example, in the child's Learning Journey (PDP/Portfolio etc.), rather than having a note or a photo of the activity with a caption that says 'Sam played with cars all day', the caption could say, 'Sam *tested out* places to find where the car would go better. Sam *used senses* to *explore*.'

The learning environment

The nursery will already be set up to support the children's social, emotional, cognitive and psychomotor development. The nursery practitioners will already be working together to maximise opportunities for learning. In order to embed metacognition they will first need to look at the metacognitive processes. (The table showing the most common target processes for the under-fives is repeated below for convenience.) They should consider what processes are happening or planned for and what is happening in the nursery to facilitate these processes. It may be that some processes will be targeted in a specific activity or area of the nursery (see Case Study 2), whereas it might be decided that others are to be made explicit as they are observed (see Case Studies 1 and 3).

looking	listening	feeling
trying out/finding out	choosing/deciding	using imagination
thinking	remembering	sharing
taking turns	wondering	keep trying

As nursery practitioners well know, at this early stage of a child's learning, it is common to respond to the individual child's interests, rather than always trying to shift them from their focus to a teacher-determined one. It is believed, for example, that the children will get far more understanding of the written communication process in the role-play corner when they choose to or see a need to pick up a pencil and start 'writing', than if they are directed away from what they are doing in order to write. Nursery practitioners are already skilled at seizing the right moment to intervene in order to facilitate learning. This skill will support those working in the nursery to recognise when is the best time to bring a metacognitive focus to the child's activity, i.e. when it is appropriate to ask the child to talk about *how they are working/playing* or to articulate what they are thinking. The metacognitive focus should be embedded according to individual need rather than in specific metacognition lessons. At appropriate times during the daily routine, the nursery practitioner can begin to make children aware of the learning skills they are using and the language that is used to describe these skills. This can be consolidated throughout the day and incorporated into other practices in the setting, as explained in more detail later in this chapter.

Case Study 2: Active outdoor play – wheeled toys

Resources: selection of wheeled toys, trikes, scooters, pedal cars
Learning intentions: gross motor skill development; to be able to control a wheeled toy; social development; to be able to share the toys
Stimulus: general nursery theme of helping others
Metacognition target: to take turns and to share

The social cooperative learning skills here serve as both learning intentions and the metacognition target. Nursery staff may just take any opportunity to emphasise the language and to praise children when they are displaying such skills.

The children are arguing over the large scooter.

Practitioner:	What do you need to do when both of you want to use the big scooter?
Child 1:	Take turns.
Practitioner:	That's right. You need to *take turns or share*. Can you both play with the scooter at the same time?
Child 2:	Yes. I can go in the front and you can go behind me.
Child 1:	I want a turn in front.
Practitioner:	Good. So you are going *to share* the scooter and *take turns* at being in front.

Case Study 3: Creative area – building houses for bears

Resources: the area will be set up with crayons, scissors, lolly sticks, tape, paper, card, hole-punch, sticks and treasury tags
Learning intentions: to show increasing control over an object and begin to use a tool effectively
Stimulus: Old Bear needs a home. Can you make a house for him?
Metacognition target: respond to children and focus on the processes each child is using to complete the task

In such activities it is helpful not to have too narrow a metacognitive focus but to respond to the child. The practitioner in the example below identifies that the child is persevering and making choices so chooses to make these processes explicit to the child.

Practitioner:	How are you making your house?
Child:	With sticks.
Practitioner:	Can you tell me a bit more about that?
Child:	I'm sticking them together for my bear.
Practitioner:	How are you doing that?
Child:	Like this (child wraps tape around a set of sticks).
Practitioner:	I see. You are using tape. What made you *choose* tape?
Child:	Tape sticks and I want them to stick together.

Practitioner returns after some time. Child is still wrapping tape round sticks.

Practitioner:	Well done! You are working hard on your house.
Child:	I am going to do a roof now.
Practitioner:	What will you choose to use for a roof?
Child:	That bit of card.
Practitioner:	What made you *choose* card?
Child:	It is flat like the roof.
Practitioner:	That's a good idea. You have had to do lots of *choosing* today. You *chose* to use sticks, then you *chose* tape because it is sticky and now you are *choosing* card for a roof. *Keep trying*. I think your house is going to be good.

Other children working in this area might offer that they are *using their imagination*, *remembering* what the bear's house in the book looked like, having a good *think*, *sharing* the scissors with the other children, etc.
Note

In older children, it is usually expected that fine and gross motor skills will already be fairly well developed as the most rapid development occurs in the early years. This means that words such as *holding carefully* or *using scissors*, for example, are not part of the metacognitive language emphasised elsewhere in this book. However, these are learning processes in younger children and it will help children become aware of how they learn if they are encouraged to think about these motor skills in addition to other learning processes. In the above example the teacher might have chosen to emphasise the child's ability to use tools to cut the tape or hold the sticks carefully while wrapping the tape, for example.

The physical environment

Once target processes have been identified, these can be incorporated into the nursery environment. The words can be displayed in relevant parts of the room accompanied by photographs or another visual image. Many of these skills can be used throughout the nursery but by displaying the word and symbol for *listen*, for example, near a listening centre or in the part of the room where children listen to the teacher or to a story, it helps the children begin to associate the language with activities in which they use listening. Initially the nursery practitioners will determine where in the room it is most appropriate for a word to be displayed, for example they may easily be able to think of areas in the room where the children most often *share* and *take turns*. If the target learning processes have not previously been a key focus of the nursery, it might be necessary for the nursery staff to have metacognition as a focus whilst observing and engaging in dialogue with the children before deciding where and how to display labels and symbols. For example, after observing *how* the children are working rather than *what* they are doing, it might become apparent that the children often use *keep trying* when building the giant railway track because it was not a simple task. Once the children have developed some awareness of the language of learning and as they begin to notice how they are carrying out tasks or what they are doing as they play, they can become more active in determining where in the room they most often use a skill or process.

I need to keep trying different ways

The labels and photographs alone do not embed the language of learning but they do provide reminders and prompts to the children and adults about what might be going on. The nursery staff can take the opportunity to ask the child to talk about the photo or the target word. They can also help the child become aware when they are using this language or engaging in these processes.

If we go back to Case Study 1, for example, there might be a photograph of the child pushing the car on the nursery floor with captions *'trying out'* and *'finding out'*. This lends itself to later discussion of the activity. The adults in the nursery might ask the child to explain what they were trying out or they might ask the other children to suggest how to try something out or to guess what Sam found out.

Photographs and captions in a nursery are very active. They are there to prompt thinking and discussion and to value the children and their achievements. Such photos and captions can easily be used to support the development of the language of learning.

Photographs might also be used as a prompt for discussion with another child engaged in a similar process. For example, a photograph from Case Study 3 could be used to help a child realise that they are able to *choose* rather than having to be told what to use. It is quite common for young children to have no experience of choosing or making decisions before they come to nursery. They expect to be told. This is an illustration of how a teacher supports a child to be aware of choices and how to choose for herself. Through learning how to make decisions she is better able to be a more independent learner. The learning conversation and process focus would be based on knowledge of the child and their individual targets. The conversation below might be appropriate for a child who was not very good at choosing or who avoided opportunities to choose.

Case Study 4: How to help a child with a particular process

The child is sitting next to the paper and pencils on a table that also has paints, crayons, card and felt.

Child: I'm doing a picture for my mum.
Practitioner: What are you going to use?
Child: I don't know. Pencils? [The child thinks there is a 'right' idea or 'correct answer' that the adult is expecting her to give.]
Practitioner: Why are you going to use pencils?
Child: I don't know … They are on the table.
Practitioner: Look at all the other things on the table. Can you see the photo of Jo making the house? Can you remember what the word next to that picture says?

The child shakes head.

Practitioner: The word next to that picture says 'choose'. Why do you think it says *choose*?
Child: Jo had to choose?
Practitioner: Jo decided to *choose*. You can *choose* what to use for the picture for your mum. What would your mum like?
Child: Lots of colours.
Practitioner: How are you going to make the colours? Are you going to *choose* paint or crayons or pencils?
Child: Mmmmm crayons. I don't like paint.
Practitioner: Well done. You are *choosing* crayons. What will you draw on?
Child: I don't know. What do I draw on?
Practitioner: You can choose paper or card or felt?

The child is silent.

Practitioner: Think about what your mum likes and what the crayons will work well on.
Child: Card?
Practitioner: Good idea. That would work well. Give it a try and see if you like how it looks.

Practicalities

It is crucial that every adult who works in the nursery is aware of the emphasis on metacognition and how this is being approached in the early years. It is much easier for an adult in the nursery to support a metacognitive approach if they understand what is meant by metacognition, why it is being used and the ways in which it is being addressed with this age group.

It is important, as with all nursery practice, to respond to the needs of the children and to build up the language and processes at an appropriate pace. Avoid flooding the room with metacognition words and labels. Instead introduce them gradually. This can be hard in settings where children attend at different times and where there are children of varying ages in the same room in any one day. It may be necessary to have laminated cards that can be moved around, rather than permanently displayed words. Some children will have more sophisticated language and may have moved on to a greater range of processes. This is where a child's profile or record of achievement can be used. The focus language and processes for each child can be identified and recorded in the profile and used in one-to-one discussions with the child when working with and looking at their profile. An example of this follows.

Tell me what you are doing in this photo?

Do you know what this word is? Why is that written there?

Can you tell me what it means to look carefully? What were you looking at? What did looking carefully help you to learn?

Is there anything else you do in nursery where you have to look carefully?

Summary and key points

This chapter discusses ways to build the foundation for a metacognitive approach to learning in young children. There is consideration of the learning environment and the role of the adults in facilitating learning conversations and promoting thinking about learning. Through practical illustrations, the chapter identifies target language for this age group and explores ways in which an early years practitioner might incorporate this language of learning into existing routines.

Learning processes included in this chapter

Process	Case Study	Process	Case Study
looking	1	feeling	1
listening		choosing/deciding	3, 4
thinking	1, 3	sharing	2, 3
taking turns	2	keep trying	1, 2
remembering	3	trying out/finding out	1
wondering	1	using imagination	3

Next steps for the reader

- Identify the main learning processes that are happening in the nursery and where they occur?
- Look for opportunities to introduce some of the language for these processes to the children in the nursery.
- Think about posting photos/words around the room to stimulate some focus on how we are learning.
- Consider ways of having 'learning conversations' with the children about how they find out about the world around them.

6 Developing a metacognitive approach in the early years (ages 4–8)

This chapter is intended to be a practical tool for teachers seeking to use a metacognitive approach. It explains how metacognition can be introduced and embedded into learning in the infant classroom. There is detailed description of an introductory activity that could be adapted for other stages of the primary school. Then, through a series of practical case studies, the chapter shows how the language of learning and a focus on how we learn can be incorporated into teaching. It uses plans for art, health and wellbeing (PSHE), science and literacy lessons as a way to explore how a metacognitive approach can be embedded into all learning.

Introduction

This chapter has been written to be accessible to those teachers with a range of experience, from students and the newly qualified to those with many years' experience of teaching in the early years. For this reason, there is a level of detail to the examples that more experienced professionals may not require. This book is all about modelling, developing and raising awareness about *how* we learn. There will be many similarities between how this looks in each age and stage of the school. However, as the learners get older and more experienced they should become much more aware and more able to articulate that awareness.

In the following section, guidance is given on how to develop metacognition with children aged between 5 and 8 years old. There is a focus on the development of metacognitive skills followed by consideration and examples on how to make metacognition explicit in lessons across the curriculum.

Introducing metacognition

Below you will find a case study called Guess My Rule. The rationale for this activity is to help children become aware of their learning and the language of learning. It is a metacognition lesson specifically intended to teach children about how they learn.

As discussed in Chapter 2, for children to engage fully in thinking and talking about their learning, they need the language with which to do so. The meta-learning word progression sheet

(Appendix 5.3) is a useful guide for working out which language or processes to consider first. Whatever the age of the children, in order to help them become more aware of the learning processes they use and to give them the language with which to discuss these processes it is necessary to start with a focus on some *processes familiar to the children*, rather than new learning.

Case Study 1: Guess My Rule activity

Resources

- two sorting hoops
- various plastic animals – different shapes, sizes and species
- various small people – a range of characters, sizes, colours, etc.
- various small vehicles – a range of sizes and colours.

Metacognition target

looking (observing)	listening
remembering	thinking
guessing which at this stage might incorporate • trying out; • making connections; • having a go; • working it out.	

When working with young children, accompanying each of these words with a physical gesture supports the children in the early stages of metacognition. It is also useful to photograph some of these visual images and display them in the room with the appropriate label, either in a specific metacognition display or in classrooms for younger children next to areas where they are likely to use these processes and skills.

It can be useful to reinforce some of the learning processes whilst also establishing a behaviour code for the activity. For example, the teacher might say that they are looking for good listening, careful looking, etc. and discuss with the children what good looking or thinking might look like and perhaps the behaviours that might suggest that a child is not listening, thinking, etc. Essentially these ground rules not only establish the learning behaviour required for the activity, but also prepare the learners for thinking about how they learn and the appropriate dispositions for learning such as listening, looking, taking turns, etc.

Interaction

Teacher:	We are going to play a game called Guess My Rule. To play the game we are going to need to be able to do these things – are you ready?
Teacher:	We need to *look* carefully (points to eyes). Can you all look? Show me good looking.

Teacher:	Brilliant! We also need *to listen* (cups ears). Are you listening? How will I know if you are listening?
Child:	Because we are sitting up straight ... etc.
Teacher:	I will know if you are listening when you are able to tell me what you have heard or if you use what you have heard to make a guess.
Teacher:	What do we need to do to be able to play the game?
Children:	We need to look and to listen. (They usually offer plenty of other suggestions like sit still, be good, etc.)
Teacher:	So we need to look, to listen and there's another thing we need to do - *think*. Do you know how to think?
Children:	Yes ... no.
Teacher:	What might we *look like* when we think?

Children offer various poses including frowns, fingers to chin, etc. Choose one to represent thinking.

I am thinking about how to make it work.

I am thinking.

Teacher:	Can you tell me when you had to think?
Children:	When I was reading, now, etc.
Teacher:	We are going to .... (points to eyes).
Children:	Look.
Teacher:	Great. Look and .... (cups ears).
Children:	Listen.
Teacher:	Well done, look, listen and .... (uses thinking gesture).
Children:	Think.

In this way, the teacher introduces the *language* and the *processes* for learning.

The next step is to explain the rules of the game. The aim is to have a rule in mind and one by one add one of the small world objects to a hoop according to that rule. It is better to demonstrate the way the game works by talking through this process once or twice and checking out the children's understanding.

It is beneficial if the teacher models by choosing the first few rules, sorting objects into hoops one at a time, emphasising the *learning skills* and the language used to describe these, getting the children to *guess the rule* and then work out where a further few objects would go. It might be a good idea to leave the more obvious rules like 'they are all big' or 'they are all small', so that the children can think of their own ideas right from the start. Once they get the hang of it they will come up with more complex suggestions for themselves.

The teacher can then hand over to a child and ask them to think of a rule. Depending on the age, ability and confidence of the child, the teacher may need to help them with this. The rules can vary from those as simple as big/small, red/not red, two legs/more than two legs to more sophisticated rules suitable for older children such as has an engine/does not have an engine, can be moved by wind/needs a fuel to move, magnetic/not magnetic.

Metacognition

Teacher acts as model to make language and processes explicit.

Teacher:	*Look* carefully. I am going to put this giraffe in the red hoop. Hmmm and now I am going to put this snake in the blue hoop. Look carefully at the giraffe and the snake and have a *think* about what the rule might be. We need more things first. Keep *looking* and *thinking*. Now I am going to put this bird in the red hoop and this snail in the blue hoop. *Look* at the animals carefully. Have a *think*. Is anyone ready to have a *try* and *guess* my rule?
Child:	The ones there are animals and those ones are not animals.
Teacher:	Good *thinking*, good guess, but that is not my rule. Look really carefully and *think* about what you see. What do the ones in the red hoop have that the ones in the blue hoop don't have?
Child:	The ones in the blue hoop don't have legs.
Teacher:	Well done! Brilliant! You *worked it out*. The rule is legs (pointing to the red hoop) and no legs (pointing to the blue hoop)!
Teacher:	Now you have to remember the rule. Look carefully and tell me where to put this next one (teacher holds up another object) and so on.

It is important to keep on using, reinforcing and drawing attention to the language of learning as the activity progresses. In this way the pupils will become more aware that these words describe and explain what it is that they do when they are learning. Just using the words is not enough; the teacher continually needs to reinforce the connection between processes and language. This can be done through using questions such as: How did you do that? How did you work out the rule? What skills did you use?

Transferable skills

Once you have moved from the basic level of rules like red/not red, etc., to counting or using known facts, there is a need to help the children realise that they are using learning from another lesson to help them solve the rule. For example they may have explored in another lesson things that float/sink. By linking this activity back to knowledge from other learning the learners begin to appreciate that learning is transferable. At this point we would not use the term *transferable* with the children, but would say something like, *remembering other learning* or *making connections*. It is important that they understand the processes involved before they are introduced to new terminology.

In addition to knowledge, it may be that they are using skills they already have, such as counting. Again, it is important to make it clear to them that they have other learning skills that they can transfer to use in new situations, like in this Guess My Rule game. In order for children to benefit from the skills that they have, they need to become aware that they are transferring skills and knowledge and applying those skills and knowledge in another setting. The language most appropriate for this is *remembering other learning* (for younger children) moving to *making connections*, and *using what I know*, or *transferring learning*, for older children.

The activity could be adapted for use with older children by increasing the skills and processes used or by making the language of learning more sophisticated. It is possible to increase the skills by having a specific subject area as a focus, for example a local history or science project: the children might sort the objects according to a rule that they have learned during their project such as lives locally, lives in another country, or is magnetic/is not magnetic.

The Guess My Rule activity can be used with older children and words like 'guess' can be replaced by words like *predict*. This brings opportunities for children to discuss their understanding of the metacognition vocabulary relevant to the particular situation.

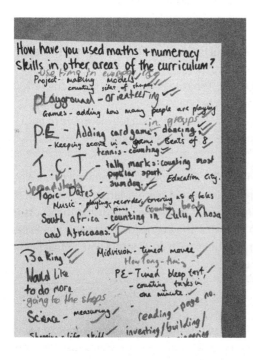
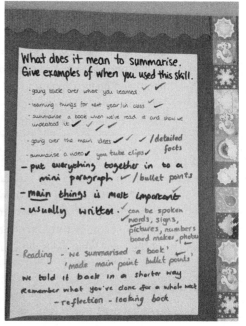

Integrating metacognition

After initial lessons such as Guess My Rule, and in conjunction with the introduction of appropriate language, it is possible to move to having a *metacognitive emphasis* in any lesson. In addition to subject specific knowledge and skills, the learning outcomes would include a focus on *the how* of learning. This would mean an increased understanding of learning, as well as the development of the vocabulary required to talk about how we learn. This is modelled in the next few activities which commonly occur in a typical primary school.

Case Study 2: Art - famous artists

Resources

- portraits by a range of artists
- art paper
- metacognition words on the classroom wall.

Learning intentions in art and metacognition

- I can respond to the work of artists and designers by discussing my thoughts and feelings. I can respond to artwork.
- I can identify a famous artist and the style of work they produce.
- I can talk about the skills I am using in my learning, using appropriate language.

Metacognition focus (any of the following processes)

looking (observing)	thinking	remembering
explaining	making connections	choosing/deciding
trying different ways	testing	solving problems

Activity

The children are going to produce a self-portrait. In this activity the children are required to consider some complex examples of self-portraits by artists such as Van Gogh, Renoir and Rembrandt and talk about what they like, dislike, what they notice. However, in order to move from appreciating and noticing elements of style, etc. to the creation of their own artwork it is first necessary to look at more simple self-portraits, such as those by Warhol, before going on to create their own self-portrait.

During each part of the lesson the teacher needs to look out for and model the use of the learning processes. The teacher should use the language of learning and emphasise when the children use the language, or identify a process appropriately. It is also important at this stage that the teacher makes sure that there is a shared understanding of the meaning of each word. For example, it can take frequent discussion before a child knows securely that testing in this context is about trying out rather than being tested or having a test.

In the first part of the lesson this might be achieved through such questions or comments as those below. Here the focus on art is supported by a focus on the metacognitive aspects of learning: thus embedding an integrated approach to *what* we learn and *how* we learn.

Look carefully. What do you notice?

Can you tell how you have been able to *notice* things by *looking* carefully?

How do you *think* Van Gogh has created his self-portrait?

I like how you have used what you can see and *connected* it with what we have done in other art lessons.

Do you *remember* how easy it was to get the shape of a face when you were sketching last week?

What do you like about it? Why? (Here the child is asked to *explain* the reasons for what they like/dislike. The teacher might comment on the learning process or apply appropriate learning words to make this more explicit to them here.)

I can tell that you have been *thinking* carefully.

Can you see how people have *listened carefully* and used what the rest of the group has said to develop their own ideas about this artist?

Metacognition

As the children move on to the second part of the lesson, in addition to supporting learning in art, the teacher is drawing out from the children, through question and answer, the target metacognitive processes in which they will be engaged. The teacher can make explicit, model and emphasise both the language and the processes, as the children

- *remember* and *think* about what they have observed or heard;
- make connections to other art work they have done (*remember other learning*);
- make decisions and *choose* which style to use for their own portrait;
- *choose and decide* what techniques or materials to use;
- *try different ways*;
- *test* ideas and approaches;
- *solve problems*.

If all the age-appropriate metacognitive language has been made available to the children in the form of wall displays or other metacognition lessons, it is important not to have too narrow a focus on the metacognitive language used and discussed in a lesson. The teacher should allow the children to suggest any learning processes they think they are using and use any vocabulary that they wish in order to try to articulate how they think they are learning. Chapter 4 explores ways of emphasising the words and processes.

For example, the key progress for one child might be that they did *not give up* until they reached a stage where they were happy with their work, whilst for another it might be that they were able to *make successful choices* on what materials to use.

A plenary might then include a focus on *how* the work has been achieved as well as *what* the children learned and achieved. At this point opportunities need to be taken to reinforce and develop the language of learning so that all have a shared understanding of the words used to describe the way we learn.

Case Study 3: Powerful verbs – literacy

Resources

- pictures of scenes from stories which demonstrate actions
- word cards
- metacognition words on the classroom wall.

Learning intentions

- I can use power words to make my writing interesting.
- I can share my ideas and listen to the opinions of others.
- I know that using imagination and trying different ways are helpful in my learning.

Metacognition focus (any of the following processes)

exploring	sharing	taking turns	showing others
trying different ways	using imagination	remembering other learning	

Activity

In this activity children are reminded about prior work on verbs. In pairs or groups they are asked to come up with some interesting/powerful *doing* words. After the introductory activities with the teacher, the children are given some pictures of scenes and word cards to create captions; they have to work in groups using word cards to build sentences that have an interesting or powerful verb. (Examples might be raced/rushed/crawled/wandered rather than went.) They will also have blank cards so that they can add more interesting words.

Teacher: I am looking for interesting sentences. *Use your imagination* and *choose* powerful verbs.

Children all start work in groups.

Teacher: What is the sentence you are making going to say?
Child A: The boy is in the park with a dog.
Child B: The boy plays in the park with his dog.
Teacher: Which sentence will you *choose*?
              Explain why you think your sentence is interesting?
              Have you *remembered* to use a powerful verb?
Child A: The boy chases round the park with his dog.
Teacher: Why did you change your sentence?

Child A: I wanted a better word than 'is' so I tried a *different way*.
Teacher: Well done. You need to keep trying different ways until you find lots of inter-
            esting sentences.

Interaction

It may be helpful to highlight the language of learning and to make explicit to the learners
how they are using and developing transferable learning skills and tools. For example, you
might enhance the above interaction with something like the following. This might be done
at the time or it might be something that you draw out in a plenary where you reflect on the
kind of learning that has taken place in the lesson.

Enhanced interaction

Which sentence will you *choose*?
Explain why you think your sentence is interesting?
Have you *remembered* to use a powerful verb?

(Then drawing the focus to metacognition:)
So you see children how you are using important learning skills.
You are making a *choice* – this involves *thinking* about which words will work best.
You are having to *explain and justify* why you chose the word.
These are very important tools to use in lots of different learning situations.
You are *remembering* to *follow instructions*, again, this is a very powerful learning
tool.
You have used some great learning tools today, well done!
(The teacher might, at the same time, draw attention to these words if they are displayed
somewhere on the classroom wall – either as pictures or images.)

Metacognition

The teacher introduces the target metacognitive processes or they can ask the children to
suggest which processes they think *they will use* in order to complete the task and achieve
the literacy outcomes. The teacher's role is to then emphasise the *processes* when observed,
either through question and answer or through comment.

Well done, you *remembered* what a verb is and you *chose* an interesting one.
Excellent, you *explained* your ideas to your group and *tried a different way* to make
the sentence more interesting.
Use your imagination now and make a different sentence.

Case Study 4: Health and Wellbeing (HWB)/Personal and Social Education (PSE) – being a good friend

Resources

- large space
- scenarios for teacher.

Learning intentions in HWB and metacognition

- I can explain what a good friend might do.
- I am aware that other people have feelings.
- I am becoming aware that sometimes my feelings can help me with my learning.

Metacognition focus (any of the following processes)

feeling	wondering	choosing/deciding
sharing	thinking	using imagination
remembering		

There could also be cooperative social learning skills.

Activity

This activity could be discussion-based in the classroom or could draw from some drama conventions in a large space such as the hall (role play, hot seating, still image, etc.). Due to the nature of the learning, it is better to have the main metacognition considerations *after the activity* in a plenary or class discussions between tasks. However, the teacher should also make the most of any opportunities to emphasise, model or make explicit a process.

The session would start with a discussion of any prior work on friends. Then the teacher reads a scenario to the children which describes the situation and perspective of a child such as the following.

Solomon's Day

I have had a horrible day. My mum had to go to work early and we were in a hurry to get to breakfast club. I was running and I tripped over my skateboard. I hurt my wrist so badly, I couldn't stop crying. I went to hospital and had an X-ray. My wrist is broken. I had to have plaster on it. I banged my head as well and so they said I had to go home and rest. I feel horrible and I am stuck at home. I was really looking forward to playing with my friend at school today but now I am in my bedroom. I can't even play on my Xbox because of my wrist and my mum is cross because she is supposed to be at work.

In groups the children discuss what they know about how Solomon is feeling. How do they know? What other feelings might he be experiencing? The teacher might intervene with questions and comments:

- I wonder how Solomon feels. I wonder how his friends would feel.
- How do you think he feels?
- Imagine what would you do?

In their groups, the children are then asked to discuss and record in a poster or act out what a group of good friends might do on hearing the news about Solomon. The teacher would determine whether role play or discussion is the most appropriate for their particular group of children. As the teacher moves around the room, they will have opportunity to ask questions, observe the learning taking place and make explicit the language of learning, in particular the focus processes for this lesson (*feel, wonder, share, choose, think, use imagination, remember*).

Once the groups have completed their poster/role play, the class can come together to share their work. At this point the teacher might put greater emphasis on the learning skills used.

Interaction with a metacognition focus

Teacher:	Tell me how your group decided on this brilliant role play.
Child:	We knew Solomon would be sad so we wanted to cheer him up.
Teacher:	How do you know he is sad?
Child:	I would be sad if it happened to me.
Teacher:	That's a good idea. You *thought* about your feelings.
Child:	I *used my imagination*. I *thought*, well if I was hurt I would be sad.
Child:	I *remembered* when Sarah had an accident. She was sad.
Child:	It made me *feel* sad when I listened to the story.
Teacher:	So you *used your feelings* to help you.

There can also be discussion of the experience of carrying out the task and consideration of how we have feelings when we learn and how these can sometimes be used as a way to learn or carry out a learning activity.

Child:	I *felt really pleased* when I was pretending to take him a present.
Child:	I *felt proud* when the others liked my idea for the poster.

Metacognition

In this HWB lesson, the teacher is helping the children become aware of their feelings and how their knowledge about feelings can support them with their learning. Although based on feelings, the lesson also requires the children to *remember* how they felt at a particular time or to *imagine* or *wonder* how they might have felt and to use this information to inform their work in this activity. They then have the opportunity to *share* their thoughts and feelings either through discussion or through role play. As this is a collaborative task, the teacher might also use it to focus on collaborative learning skills such as *considering others*, *being a good team member*.

Case Study 5: Science - electric circuits

Resources

- concept cartoons (Naylor and Keogh 2000)
- battery packs
- wires with crocodile clips
- light bulbs.

Learning intentions in science

- I can describe what makes a simple electric circuit.
- I can construct a simple electric circuit.
- I know that learning in science sometimes includes making suggestions and working with others to solve science.

Metacognition focus (any of the following processes)

Part 1

remembering other learning	listening to the opinions of others	thinking
suggesting	looking	explaining reasons
having a go	working out	wondering

Part 2

working out	testing	exploring
thinking	problem solving	trying different ways
keep trying	cooperating	being a good team member

Unless the children are confident with metacognition, it is probably better to have only some of these processes and associated vocabulary as a target focus during the activity, whilst allowing the children to introduce more if they recognise them.

Part 1

Give the children a concept cartoon (Naylor and Keogh 2000) showing a simple electric circuit, for example one in which there is an error and the light bulb does not light up. The cartoon should include suggestions in speech bubbles on why it does not light up.

The children in their groups should discuss the cartoon, the suggestions and *explain their own reason* for the circuit not working, giving justification.

Either prior to or during the discussion, the teacher can bring to the children's attention or ask them to identify what *learning processes they are using* in the activity. In Chapter 4 we look at ways to involve the children in identifying the learning processes as they work.

Part 2

Once this discussion period is over, the group can then collect the resources required to make the circuit from the cartoon, acting on the suggestions discussed in order to fix the error and make the bulb light up. At this point, the learning focus has moved to *working out, testing, exploring, thinking, solving a problem* and if necessary *to keep trying and try different ways*. The teacher may need to make the children aware of the change of skills by asking them about how they are learning now or this may be better as an extension to the lesson (see below). It may be relevant to have cooperative learning skills emphasised here or it may be more appropriate to leave those for another activity, depending on how new the children are to metacognition.

Metacognition

The teacher's role is to model the process while the children are engaged, for example with comments and questions such as:

> I can see that you are *thinking* and *working out*.
> How did you *solve the problem*?
> Well done. You *remembered* the circuit work we did last week.
> Can you *try a different way*?
> How do you know? What skills did you use?
> Why don't you *explore* what happens if you do ....

It may be helpful to highlight the language of learning and to make explicit to the learners how they are using and developing transferable learning skills and tools. The teacher can seize opportunities to do this while the children work. This might also be achieved during a plenary in which the children reflect on the kind of learning that has taken place in the lesson.

The teacher might ask questions such as:

> What do we know now about electric circuits?
> How do we know this?
> Look at the words in our language of learning display. What processes did you use? What strengths did you bring to your group?

Or individual skills can be targeted:

What part of this activity needed you to *work out/think/solve problems*?
Describe how you *worked it out/explored/tried different ways*.

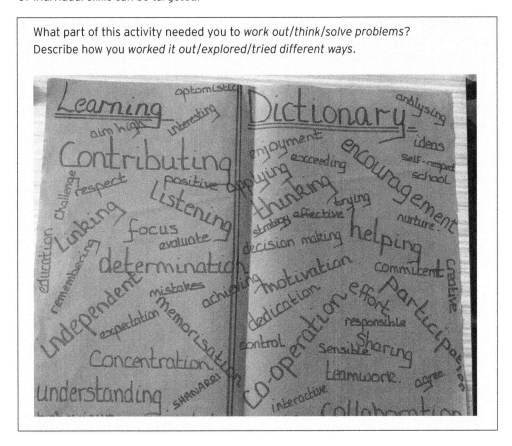

Extension to Case Study 5

It is possible to return to an activity such as the science one, once metacognition is firmly integrated into classroom practice. At this point, a metacognitive conversation can be held with questions like:

1   Which learning processes change when you move from the discussion to action?
2   In what ways do these processes change when you move from the discussion to action?
3   Which processes do you find easiest?
4   Which processes do you find most difficult?
5   Do you have some children in your group who already have useful approaches to learning that help the group?
6   Does the group depend on anyone in particular for these useful approaches to learning that help the group?

It is useful to make the children aware of these issues and to involve them in suggesting how to move forward.

Summary and key points

In this chapter we have used case studies to demonstrate how to develop a metacognitive approach with children aged between 5 and 8 years old. The first case study focuses on introducing the concept of metacognition to the children through a game called Guess My Rule, which can also be adapted for use as an introductory task for older children. Within each, target learning processes are identified alongside subject-based learning intentions. Case Studies 2–5 look at how an emphasis on learning processes can be embedded within lessons on art, literacy, health and wellbeing (PHSE) and science.

Learning processes included in this chapter

Process	Case Study	Process	Case Study	Process	Case Study
looking	1, 2, 5	solving problems	2, 5	cooperating	5
listening	1, 5	working out	1, 5	feeling	4
thinking	1, 2, 4, 5	wondering	4, 5	sharing	3, 4
remembering	1, 2, 4	exploring	3, 5	taking turns	3
remembering other learning	1, 3, 5	being a good team member	5	keep trying	5
having a go/guessing/ trying out	1, 5	showing others	3	trying different ways	2, 3, 5
explaining	2, 3, 5	suggesting	5	testing	2, 5
choosing/deciding	1, 3, 4, 5	using imagination	3, 4		

Next steps for the reader

- Consider how you might introduce the concept of metacognition to your class.
- Look at your existing plans, identify how the children will be learning and how they will achieve the learning intentions. This is not *what* they do but *how*; the skills they will need.
- You may wish to use the Case Study examples 2–5 for suggestions on how to embed a metacognitive approach into some of your lesson plans.

Reference

Naylor, S. and Keogh, B. (2000) *Concept Cartoons in Science Education*. Sandbach: Millgate House Publishers.

7 Developing a metacognitive approach in the middle years (ages 8–10)

> This chapter is intended to be a practical tool for teachers seeking to use a metacognitive approach. It explains how metacognition can be introduced and embedded into learning in the lower junior classroom, but strategies could be adapted for any age. There is a reminder of some of the benefits of introducing this approach in the first example. Then, through a series of practical case studies, the chapter shows how the language of learning and a focus on how we learn can be incorporated into teaching. It uses plans for science, music and literacy lessons as a way to explore how a metacognitive approach can be embedded into all learning.

Introduction

Ownership of learning and understanding of how to learn are considered to be ways of helping children have more confidence and independence as learners. Research currently being carried out in Scotland has found that many teachers see metacognition as a crucial way to develop their pupils' self-confidence and self-esteem, promoting positive mental health which in turn underpins success in learning. This chapter seeks to show some of the ways in which a focus on thinking about learning can be put in place during lessons and as part of the culture and ethos of the classroom. This book is all about modelling, developing and raising awareness about *how* we learn. There will be many similarities between how this looks in each age and stage of the school.

In the following section, guidance is given on how to develop metacognition with children aged between 8 and 10 years old. There is a focus on the development of metacognitive skills followed by consideration and examples on how to make metacognition explicit in lessons across the curriculum.

Creating a culture for metacognition

Case Study 1: The good learner

Learning intentions

- I am learning about how I learn and how to be a good learner.
- I am learning about what I need to do to be a good learner.

In order for children to think and talk about their learning, there may need to be a change in the culture and ethos of the classroom. This might involve a discussion at the beginning of the year on what a good learner is. This may appropriately form part of Rights Respecting Schools aims. However, whilst valuing a need for all learners to respect each other, it is important to make sure that the description of a good learner is not entirely formed by latent behaviour management strategies.

Teacher:	What do you think a good learner is like?
Child:	They sit still and put their hand up?
Child:	They don't talk when you are talking?
Teacher:	Well that certainly helps make sure that they are not disruptive to other people's learning but it doesn't tell us anything about learning itself. What will be going on in a good learner's head? What might they be thinking or feeling?

There are many collaborative learning skills valuable to the learning process and crucial to a positive learning environment. However, there is a danger of a discussion on learning becoming all about these social skills. The teacher needs to help the children to come up with a picture of a learner that addresses positive behaviour, collaborative skills and respect for others, but one that has at its heart attitudes and skills fundamental to being an informed, confident and independent learner. This is best done through small discussion groups that feed back into the whole class group at a later stage. The example below is probably one familiar to most teachers and is intended to illustrate the kind of dialogue required in order to create a picture of a good learner.

Teacher:	What will be going on in a good learner's head? What might they be thinking or feeling?
Child:	They will be thinking about their work.
Teacher:	Good. A good learner will be thinking about *how* to do their work. We will think about some of the ways we learn later in the lesson. Let's have a quick think now about how a good learner might be feeling.
Child:	Determined.
Child:	Confident.
Teacher:	They are great attitudes towards learning and they will help you if you are struggling. What do you do when you are stuck on a piece of work?
Child:	Ask for help.
Child:	Try another way.
Child:	Worry.
Teacher:	It is a very positive thing to ask for help and try another way. What would you be worried about?
Child:	Getting it wrong.
Teacher:	What happens when you get it wrong?
Child:	You help me work out how to do it another way.

> Teacher: So it's not the end of the world if you are stuck or get something wrong. It is a part of learning. If you know how you learn, you might get even better at solving problems for yourself.

The teacher is trying to lead the children towards an understanding that a good learner

- takes responsibility for their own learning;
- has growing confidence;
- knows when to ask for help and how to solve problems independently;
- understands and is able to explain how they are learning;
- knows that there is always more to learn;
- is not afraid of having a try and making a mistake;
- understands that you can learn from having a try, from not getting it right first time and that there are usually many different ways to achieve the same thing;
- knows that challenge is good; if you get everything right all the time, that might mean you are not learning.

There will be other characteristics and attitudes relevant to the class. The outcome of the session should be that children have discussed what it is to be a learner and have perhaps shifted away from more behaviour-oriented conceptions. The profile of a good learner can be displayed in the classroom and used as a reminder.

With younger classes you might create a character to represent the good learner: 'Lexi the learner' might be created by drawing around one of the children and then put on a wall display. Words can be written to label what might be going on in his/her head during a challenging learning activity. The teacher can then draw attention to Lexi from time to time: 'What would Lexi do here?' or 'Do you think Lexi would give up like that? What might he/she do instead?'

Metacognition

It would be appropriate at the end of the lesson to explore how they worked out what a good learner was. They might be able to identify that they used the following processes or skills:

thinking	listening to the opinions of others	considering others
deciding	explaining their own thoughts and feelings	trying out ideas
working out	making connections and using experience to make suggestions	revising or retrying

Embedding the culture

The profile of a good learner will need to be supported by actions and behaviours that reinforce these characteristics, for example language and responses that support the culture of having a try and learning through error. There should be immersion in the language of learning with a culture of talking about learning. There could be strategies or a structure in place that gives children the experience of taking responsibility for their learning, for example providing differentiated tasks but supporting the child to choose which one is appropriate for them or providing a means through which children can identify additional support needs or areas in which they would like more challenge.

Illustration – self-selected tasks

Teacher:	There are four maths activities today. Each one uses a different set of skills and you may need to have some skills before you can do a task. Look at the tasks and see which one you think you can do. Try to find one that you have the right skills for but that will still be a challenge.
Teacher:	Why have you chosen this one?
Child:	Because I know I can do it.
Teacher:	Will you learn anything new if you can already do it?
Child:	Mmmm I don't know.
Teacher:	Look at the next task. What do you need to be able to do to tackle that one? Why don't you give it a try?
Child:	What if I get it wrong?
Teacher:	What do you think will happen?
Child:	You'll be cross?
Teacher:	I will be pleased with you for having a try. What do we need to look for if you get it wrong?
Child:	The right way?
Teacher:	How do we find another way?
Child:	Look at how I did it. Think about it and see if I can work out what I did wrong.
Teacher:	Great and that way you will have a challenge and learn something new.
Teacher:	Why have you chosen this one?
Child:	I think I can do it quickly and then go onto the next one.
Teacher:	Can you say a bit more about that?
Child:	I am not sure I can do the third task but I think if I do this one first it will remind me about addition and subtraction and then I think I will be able to do the next one.
Teacher:	That sounds like you know what you need.

Metacognition and learning have a symbiotic relationship: metacognition supports and unlocks learning, and learning supports and develops metacognition. The children have to understand how they learn in order to benefit most from such an environment but such an environment is one of the ways to help children develop a greater understanding of how they learn and this knowledge can help them to learn more or better.

It takes time to build up the environment, language and ways of behaving that create this positive learning culture. It will be important to try to embed the focus on how to learn into all lessons in a meaningful way. With some children that might be helping them identify what skills and strategies they use each time; with other children it might be more about helping them to use their knowledge of themselves as a learner to help them apply appropriate skills and strategies to a learning task.

The following case studies assume a positive learning culture. They take as their basis general teaching activities and seek to illustrate how to embed thinking and talking about learning meaningfully in ways that support the learning.

Case Study 2: Science - changing states of water

Resources

- poster paper
- paper or electronic picture of landscape showing land, water, clouds and sun
- the language of the water cycle (on cards, electronically or on wall display)
- water, kettle, saucepan lid.

Learning intentions in science and metacognition

- I know that water changes state and can explain what happens.
- I can use my knowledge of how water changes state to begin to understand some of the processes involved in the water cycle.
- I can explain how I have applied previous learning about water to learn in a new context.

Metacognition focus (any of the following processes)

noticing	making and justifying predictions	making connections and using other learning
explaining	deciding	testing

Activity

The children have already done practical work with water: watching what happens when water boils, observing the water vapour and condensation. In this lesson they are asked to refresh what they know by briefly working in groups to create a poster that explains and labels the changing state of water. They will then be presented with a picture of a landscape and asked to use their knowledge of the changing states of water to explain what happens with the natural water cycle. They have to solve this problem in groups and can present their understanding in the form of a poster, electronic presentation or a role-play weather forecast. Some children may need to revisit the prior learning practically so there should be supervised access to some freshly boiled water in a container over which a lid can temporarily be placed.

As the science learning intention is demanding application of knowledge, there is a great deal of overlap between this and the metacognition learning intention in which the teacher helps the children to be aware of how they use and apply existing knowledge. It would be appropriate for the teacher to make clear to the children that the skill is in making connections to and applying prior learning, as children can sometimes disengage because 'We've done this before!' The children will benefit from being made aware of how often prior knowledge can be used and how crucial this is to the learning process. The use of models in science relies on the child's ability, facilitated by the teacher, to make the connection between the model and the real world.

After the children have worked in their groups to remind themselves of what they learned in the previous lesson, the teacher should bring the focus back to the process of learning.

Teacher:	What did we learn about water last week?
Child:	When you boil it, it turns to a gas.
Child:	When the steam cools down it turns back into water.
Teacher:	How did we learn it?
Child:	We used water and we watched to see what happened.
Teacher:	Last week we made predictions and we noticed what was happening. We used science words such as 'gas' to describe what was happening.

Other processes can be acknowledged and it would be appropriate to collect the scientific language used for the current lesson. The teacher should then introduce what the children need to do next in their groups. This should be followed by a discussion of how they will achieve the learning. This may be a familiar process to children who are used to understanding what the success criteria of a lesson are before they start.

Teacher:	This week we are going to learn in a different way. You will need to be science detectives.
	You are going to need lots of skills. You have managed the first one already. You have *remembered* what you learnt last week. Now I need you to *use that knowledge* and *apply* it to a problem.
	How do you *think* what you know about water changing will help you work out what happens with the weather? What is the *connection*?
	Explain your ideas to each other and come up with a suggestion or hypothesis. Don't just guess. I need you to *think and be able to explain* your ideas.

At this point it is important to check that the children have a clear understanding of the metacognition vocabulary. With the current emphasis on collaborative learning, children often hear the phrase *making connections* and think of establishing friendships; alternatively they may assume a more practical meaning of physically joining up objects. Ideally there should be an ongoing focus on the language so that it is established in the classroom, as to introduce new metacognition language in a lesson where science is the ultimate learning intention might just be too much for some children. Time allocated to learning journals and reflection or metacognition activities such as Guess My Rule (see Chapter 6) or Reading the Impossible (see Chapter 8) are useful for this.

During the group work the teacher needs to be looking for the target learning processes and engaging children in conversations about how they are learning. This dialogue needs to support the science learning but also help the children have an explicit understanding of how they are learning. Some children may be able to apply the prior learning with confidence. Others may need to redo a part of the practical work to deepen their understanding. It is important (health and safety considerations addressed) that opportunities are provided for the children to observe again water changing states.

This is a useful learning process, a recognition that sometimes we need to check or revisit to get a true understanding or that sometimes we think we understand until we go to apply the knowledge and then we realise there are gaps in our understanding. This is the iterative cycle of knowing, applying, having more questions, checking and testing new knowledge, re-applying and coming to a stronger understanding of the prior learning and its meaning in the new context. This cyclical process is best supported by an environment which places emphasis on trying and the process rather than just on outcomes and 'correct' answers.

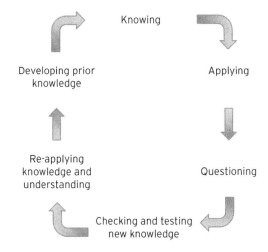

Figure 7.1 The iterative learning cycle

Case Study 3: Music – exploring texture

Resources

- clips of music – progressing from solo unaccompanied instrumental music to a band with a defined bass line, drumming pattern, rhythm guitar, lead guitar and lead singer
- classroom percussion instruments.

Learning intentions in music and metacognition

- I can use my voice and musical instruments to experiment with sounds, melody, rhythm and timbre.
- I am becoming aware that the musical dimension of *texture* is how the melodic, rhythmic and harmonic materials are combined to create the overall quality of the sound in a composition.
- I can explain how I am learning and how I am developing my musical skills.

Metacognition focus (any of the following processes)

listening	using prior or new learning	deciding
noticing patterns	being a good team member	revising

Activity

The lesson starts with the children listening to a selection of recorded music. This is followed by a discussion of the different levels of complexity. The teacher then demonstrates how the children can follow different rhythm patterns and the children then go on to create their own patterns. As a group they explore how layers can be built up from a single voice to everyone playing and reduced gradually back to a single voice.

In the second part of the lesson the children work in small groups to create their own compositions that demonstrate different timbres, volumes and textural complexity, using vocal and body sounds in addition to classroom percussion instruments. The lesson concludes with a performance for their peers from whom they receive feedback.

Metacognition

In this lesson it is appropriate for the teacher to share the focus learning processes at the start in addition to other success criteria. This helps the children to be aware from the outset of how they can achieve the intended learning and participate fully in the activities. This might be done through questioning as illustrated below.

Teacher: You are going to learn how to hear and then create a piece of music that has different levels of complexity. That sounds very tricky doesn't it? How do you think we are going to manage to do something so grown up?

Child: Do what you tell us.

Teacher: You may start by *listening* to me and copying me. That would be a good start, but you will need to do more if you want to understand how to create complex music. What else might you need to do?

Child: Play instruments.

Child: Make a rhythm.

Child: Keep together.

Teacher: Good. At one point I will ask you to use musical instruments and to do that you will need to *remember how* to play them and all the other skills and facts that you know about those instruments. You will also need to *remember* what we have learned already in our music lessons and *use* that to help you today. Before we move on, is there anything else anyone wants to say about *how* they think we will learn today?

Child: Try hard.

> Teacher: That's a great attitude to have. If you try hard I am sure you will do really well. So in this first part of our music lesson today, you need to *listen*. There will also be lots of *thinking*. You really need to think about what you are listening to and *listen out for patterns* and other features; you will need to *use what you have heard and what you learned* about music from listening to make your own patterns.

The teacher is trying to put emphasis on the following processes so that the children are clear of what is required:

- listening;
- thinking about what you hear;
- looking for patterns in what you hear;
- using what you have heard and noticed to make your own composition.

This discussion also makes it clear how complex a process listening is and how thinking and other mental processes such as pattern identification can all be expected within what might seem to be 'just' a listening task.

The first part of the lesson is teacher directed. The teacher should take every opportunity to reinforce the learning processes alongside the music learning. This could be done through positive recognition. For example, by saying: 'Well done. You listened carefully and noticed when the number of sounds was getting smaller again'. As the children become more skilled at metacognition, they may be able to identify and record for themselves how they are learning, perhaps through use of cards, recording on a metacognition display or on a laminated sheet. See Chapter 4 for more detail on such strategies.

As they move on to the second part of the lesson, the teacher needs to help the children to be aware of how they have achieved the first part in addition to what they have done. The teacher needs to make clear what skills, learning processes and knowledge from the first part will be employed in the second. The group work also requires collaborative learning skills and these might also be emphasised as part of the usual behaviour management strategies. The teacher will also need to engage in dialogue with individual groups to support the learning. A focus on the how of learning will be an important part of these conversations.

Interaction

> Teacher: How are you using what you know already about music?
> Child: We know music can have lots of layers.
> Teacher: Can you tell me a bit more about the layers?
> Child: Different things are happening at the same time and sometimes there are just a few things happening. Everybody doesn't always stop at the same time.
> Teacher: How have you used this knowledge in your composition?

| Child: | Christopher and Sophie are playing the same rhythm on the triangle and drum at the same time but after a bit Katherine and Joshua start singing. Then Katherine and Joshua stop but Christopher and Sophie carry on. |
| Teacher: | Well done. I can see that you have *used what you know* to work out how to layer your composition. |

With another group the teacher might use a focus on metacognition to intervene when things are not going so smoothly. Often it is the processes of learning that are inhibiting a task rather than the knowledge and understanding.

Teacher:	Tell me what you are doing here.
Child:	We are doing a composition with the glock and our voices.
Teacher:	How is it going?
Child:	Tracy keeps playing at the wrong time.
Teacher:	How do you know it is the wrong time?
Child:	Because that's when I am playing.
Teacher:	What do you all need to do to be able to perform this piece?
Child:	Tell the others what to do.
Teacher:	This is a group task. You are *working together*.
Child:	We need to listen to each other.
Teacher:	Yes. *Listen* and *work out* together what you want and how to achieve it. That way everyone will know what they are working towards. *Listen* to each other and to the music. Talk about the patterns you want to make and how you will make them. Make sure you all understand what you want to do. You will need to *keep trying* and you may need to *revise* or change things if they do not work.

The lesson ends with a performance. This provides opportunity to discuss the feeling and thoughts of those performing and those responding. The children are to give each other feedback. It might be appropriate to ask them to comment on how they achieved the per-formed composition as well as on their emotional response and thoughts about what they have heard. Feedback should be based on learning intentions. However, as within all the expressive arts, there should be recognition of and space to voice an emotional response. Prompts for feedback might include:

- How did it make you feel?
- What did you notice about the music?
- How did you notice this?
- How do you think they achieved this composition?
- What knowledge about music do you think they used?

Case Study 4: Literacy - speaking and listening

Resources

- sound clips of children's speeches or scripts of speeches for children to read out
- critical listening grid.

Learning intentions in literacy and metacognition

- I can show my understanding of what I listen to including drawing inferences.
- I can distinguish fact from opinion.
- I am learning to recognise when my sources try to influence me.
- I am aware of the skills I need to listen critically.

Metacognition focus (any of the following processes)

applying experience or learning	expressing thoughts	making an informed choice and justifying decisions
listening critically	working out/evaluating	thinking

Activity

In this lesson the children have to listen critically to a series of speeches by children standing for election as school council or eco council representative. The speeches in this case are not real ones but the aim of the critical listening is to help the children be aware of what is going on in persuasive speech so that they can make informed choices. A consolidation lesson might be for them to devise their own persuasive speeches. The children's attention will also be brought to the similarity between this situation and that of political candidate speeches.

The lesson begins with a class discussion on the purpose of a speech by someone trying to be elected in a school role. The children are reminded of some of the strategies of critical listening:

- Work out the speaker's message.
- Consider the speaker and their motivation.
- Listen to the content and evaluate evidence for the claims made. What words are they using?
- How is the speaker doing this? Is the speaker selling themselves or attacking someone else?

The children then listen to a selection of speeches, making notes using the strategies as a framework. They then have to decide who they would vote for and why. The learning about listening could be extended by an additional task in which after making the first decision, each speaker could be given a name and a character description, details about their actions and behaviours. The children could then listen again with this information in mind and see if their opinions change, discussing why they have changed.

A metacognitive focus in this lesson can be what ensures that the children actually achieve the learning outcomes rather than just making random guesses to complete the task. It would be helpful for the teacher to start the lesson by drawing out how the children can achieve the task. It is as useful to think of the learning processes they are not using as well as those that they are:

> Teacher: How are you going to use the speeches to help you make a decision?
> Child: I am going to *listen* to what they say.
> Teacher: You will listen and then how will you use what you have heard?
> Child: I'll listen and *guess* whether they would do a good job.
> Teacher: Guessing is sometimes useful but is there a better strategy you could use in this task?

The teacher acknowledges that we do guess at times, but for this lesson there needs to be a different process.

> Teacher: You are detectives looking for clues. *Listen* out for information about the person, what they will do and how they will do it. *Think* about what you hear. Does it make sense? Use what you have heard to *make your decision*.

It may be appropriate to *consider* each critical listening strategy in turn and *work out* how to *make an informed choice*.

Critical listening strategy	Learning process
Work out the speaker's message.	Listen, think, draw on prior knowledge, identify key points.
Consider the speaker and their motives.	Use knowledge about the speaker and why they are speaking.
Listen to the content and evaluate evidence for the claims made: what words are they using?	Listen, think, consider the key points in relation to what you already know (make connections). Listen out for proof that they can do what they are claiming.
How is the speaker doing this: is the speaker selling themselves or attacking someone else?	Evaluate what you hear and use prior knowledge to work out what kind of speech it is. Consider your own feelings: how does it make you feel about the speaker?

Throughout the listening task, the teacher can remind the children what they should be using to help them make their choice. This can be done through intervention or by use of visual reminders of the learning processes involved.

When the children have to explain who they would vote for and why, it might be useful for the teacher to draw their attention to the skills they use here. They are *expressing their thoughts* or *feelings* and justifying their decision. This means that they cannot randomly pick a name but instead have to persuade their listeners that they have a reason for their choice and justify that. If the children are working in the kind of positive learning environment discussed in Case Study 1, there should be an acceptance of individual difference. This should allow children to have the confidence to justify their choices even if they hear that others have chosen differently.

Transferable skills

The lesson could conclude with a consideration of what they have learned and how critical listening can help them in the world outside school. The children may already see the connection to political elections, but if not they can be prompted to. The children may also be able to identify other areas where they hear speakers trying to influence choices, such as in advertising or peer pressure situations.

Teacher:	How can you make an informed decision?
Child:	Don't guess.
Child:	*Listen and think*.
Child:	*Remember* what you already know.
Child:	*Work out* what they want.

Summary and key points

In this chapter we have highlighted the importance of embedding a metacognitive approach within a positive learning environment. Case Study 1 considers how to create a shared understanding of *the good learner*. There is emphasis on the need for learners to be aware that they need to have ownership of their learning. There is discussion of how to create a classroom ethos that ensures that this vision of the good learner is supported and reinforced by actions and behaviours in the classroom. This includes consideration of strategies to help children take greater ownership of their learning. Case Studies 2–4 look at how an emphasis on learning processes can be embedded within lessons on science, music and literacy. Within these case studies, target learning processes are identified alongside subject-based learning intentions.

Learning processes included in this chapter

Process	Case Study	Process	Case Study	Process	Case Study
noticing/observing	2	solving problems	2	concentrating	2
listening	3, 4	looking for patterns	3	being a good team member	3
testing or trying out	1, 2, 3	checking	2	planning	2, 3
expressing feelings and thoughts	1, 3, 4	redrafting	1	exploring	2, 3
improving, revising, retrying	1, 3	considering others	1, 3	thinking	1, 2, 3, 4
making connections/ remembering other learning	1, 2, 3, 4	working out	2, 3, 4	deciding	1, 2, 3, 4
justifing predictions or decisions	2, 4	applying experience or learning	1, 2, 3, 4	listening to the opinions of others	1, 2, 3, 4

Next steps for the reader

- Consider how you might introduce the concept of metacognition to your class.
- Does your class have a shared understanding of what is expected of a good learner and how to be a good learner?
- Look at your existing plans: identify how the children will be learning and how they will achieve the learning intentions. This is not *what* they do, but *how*, i.e. the skills they will need.
- You may wish to use the Case Study examples 2–4 for suggestions on how to embed a metacognitive approach into some of your lesson plans.

8 Developing a metacognitive approach in the upper years (ages 10–13)

This chapter is intended to be a practical tool for teachers seeking to use a meta-cognitive approach. It explains how metacognition can be introduced and embedded into learning in the upper years classroom. The case studies are designed to heighten pupils' awareness of metacognition by making them think about how they learn. In the case study examples, pupils are encouraged to use appropriate language to articulate their process. Sample interactions illustrate the importance of the teacher's role in facilitating dialogue and encouraging thought. Case Study 5 focuses on how to help pupils identify transferable skills.

Introduction

This book is all about modelling, developing and raising awareness about *how* we learn. There will be many similarities between how this looks in each age and stage of the school. However, as the learners get older and more experienced they should become much more aware and more able to articulate that awareness. With older pupils as the focus, this chapter explores how to plan for metacognitive interactions and how to capitalise on the incidental interactions that arise during teaching.

There is a need to plan for metacognition in ways similar to that illustrated in the case studies of Chapters 6 and 7. In addition to planned interventions, the teacher in the upper years classroom also needs to be looking out for any opportunities that arise to highlight and make explicit the metacognitive awareness of the pupils. Whether these opportunities arise spontaneously or as a result of activities set up with metacognition in mind it is the role of the teacher to model, develop and make explicit, 'the *way* we are learning'.

This ongoing focus on how the pupils are learning can be consolidated in regular opportunities to discuss learning, how they learn and how they can use what they know about learning to learn better. These discussions should help pupils to identify and reflect on *how* they learn, not *what* they are doing. It can take pupils quite some time to get to grips with this distinction between *how* and *what*. This process can be supported through prompt questions that focus their learning reflections. Whilst there is no limit to the potential open-ended questions that could be used and it is better for them to be responsive, it can be useful to have a list of prompt questions to guide these conversations.

- How did you get on?
- What did you do?
- What was hard? Why?
- What was easy? Why?
- Which skills did you use?
- What do you learn about your own learning skills here?
- Where else might you use these skills?

The language of learning needs to become a part of the classroom culture. The teacher may initially need to use a great deal of positive reinforcement in order to raise the profile of the *language of learning*. It is also essential to make sure that everyone has a shared understanding of what each term means. As the teacher becomes more aware of the pupils' understanding of how they learn, it will probably be appropriate to plan specific lessons or activities to develop or make explicit certain learning skills.

The following case studies describe a number of activities that hold the potential for rich learning conversations. It is important, though, to remember that these activities are the *vehicle for metacognition*: the activities themselves do not really matter. The activities could be substituted by something else – it is the pedagogy and the raising of awareness about the *language of learning* that is the key element.

Case Study 1: Reading the impossible

Resources

- copies of the 'Reading the Impossible' text.

Learning intentions (including for metacognition)

- I am learning about how to make sense of an unfamiliar text.
- I am learning about how to describe the skills and strategies I need to make sense of a text.

Metacognition focus (any of the following processes)

looking (observation)	thinking	making connections
guessing	trying out	solving problems

Activity

> *Reading the impossible*
>
> In'st it isetnreintg taht wehn the lterets in a wrod are in the wonrg oderr yuo can aula-clty slitl uesdtannrd waht yur'oe rdnaieg.
> Htis mkeas you tinhk aoubt how yuo raed as wlel as wtah you raed.
> It dseno't mttaer in waht oderr the lterets in a wrod are yuo can laenr mroe aoubt teh srtageits yuo use to wrok out ufmarialin wrods.

The pupils, as individuals, attempt to make sense of the text. Then, working in groups, they consider what strategies they each used and why, and compare their approaches to the task. They are thinking and talking about *how* they read and not *what* the words say. This might result in the pupils being able to draw up a list of reading strategies for any reading task.

In order for the focus to remain on the process of learning, the teacher will need to monitor the groups and engage pupils in learning conversations. This could be reinforced during a plenary discussion.

Teacher:	How did you get on?
Pupil:	I was confused at first we thought it was a foreign language.
Teacher:	What did you do?
Pupil:	We looked along the line to see if we recognised any of the words.
Teacher:	What was hard? Why?
Pupil:	It was tricky at first because they were spelt all wrong.
Teacher:	What was easy? Why?
Pupil:	After a bit we just tried to read it fast and somehow we were able to read it!
Teacher:	Which skills did you use?
Pupil:	Well we were reading and using what we knew about how to sound out the words. We also knew it needed to make sense.
Teacher:	Did you use any other skills?
Pupil:	We were also helping each other to problem solve.
Pupil:	Yes, we were guessing and agreeing and checking our ideas while we were doing it.
Pupil:	Yes and we had to review it at the end to check it made sense.
Teacher:	What do you learn about your own learning skills here?
Pupil:	Well we had a system and a plan.
Pupil:	We were able to keep trying and not give up.
Pupil:	We used what we knew about reading and were able to use this to help us.
Teacher:	Where else might you use these skills?
Pupil:	Anywhere really. Any situation where there is a problem to be solved and someone to work with to solve it. It might also help us when we are trying to read new or tricky words – you still need to look at the beginning letter, sound it out and then check if it makes sense.
Pupil:	Yes and looking at the whole sentence also helped to see if it made sense. I was amazed that we could actually read it at all!

In this dialogue, you can see that the pupils are not only talking about how they read but also they are identifying transferable skills, processes, strategies and attitudes applicable to all learning. This distinction could be made explicit to the pupils, depending on the learning intentions of the lesson and the individual need of the pupils in each group.

Metacognition

In this activity the pupils were caught up in the mystery of the problem solving. They used what they knew about literacy and word analysis to begin to decode each word. Very soon they were able to focus less on each specific word and allow the flow of the sentence to guide them.

The metacognitive questions at the end enabled them to recognise and acknowledge that they had used learning skills on this task and that these skills might be useful in other areas of their learning in different situations. It is interesting to note the social skills and collaborative skills that were also identified here: helping each other, agreeing, checking, working it out, not giving up.

The activity puts the focus on the how of reading - which is a key aspect of metacognition. By doing the activity and then thinking about how they learned they could become more aware of how they go about reading new texts, and therefore think about how to learn better.

Case Study 2: Crossing the swamp

Resources

- large open space (gym or outside)
- hoops
- mats
- cones as markers for swamp.

Learning intentions

The learning intentions for this activity are PE based but also include collaborative learning and metacognition:

- I can work together with others to find a solution.
- I can improve my range of physical skills (PE).
- I can choose, adapt and apply physical movement skills and strategies with control to achieve a goal (PE).
- I can explain how I have set out to achieve a goal.

Metacognition focus (any of the following processes)

working out	working together	making decisions
thinking	listening to others	remembering other learning
planning ahead - predicting what might happen	trying out	making improvements

Activity

This is a practical activity, best done outside or in a big space like a gym hall. The class is divided into groups. Each group has three small hoops or mats as stepping stones. There is a clearly defined swamp zone in the space. The challenge for each group is to get their whole team and all of the equipment across the swamp without touching the floor. The swamp is too wide to jump across or to throw the stepping stones across. The group will need to discover the best way to work as a team in order to get across. There is emphasis on collaborative skills and on applying what they already know about passing objects and moving safely.

This lesson demands responsiveness from the teacher, who will be supporting the pupils throughout to work as a team and to focus on *how* they will achieve the goal and solve the problem. It might be useful to look at the target metacognitive processes, or to get the pupils to identify them, so that the pupils are aware that the way to achieve the task is to think carefully about how they will do so. The teacher may need to stop the whole class or interact with individual groups if they see that the pupils are not pausing to think and plan.

Teacher:	Now let's all just stop and think: tell me what you are doing and what is in your head?
Pupil:	Well I think we need to throw the things out like stepping stones and then run across but they won't listen to me.
Pupil:	But if she does that then we will be over there and the stuff will still be in the swamp.
Teacher:	Good so you are *predicting* what will happen. What else do you need to do?
Pupil:	We need a plan first before we do anything daft!
Teacher:	So you are thinking now about some of the learning skills that will help you. You need to *think*, and to *discuss*, and to *plan* and most of all, you need to *work together*. Now, without touching the equipment for the next 5 minutes you need to *decide* just what you are going to do and who will do it.

Metacognition

Allowing the groups to forge ahead like this first of all before stopping them makes the meta-learning all the more obvious. Through the experience of not getting it right or of blundering ahead without a plan or by arguing about what is to happen makes the teacher intervention necessary and beneficial. This is supported by a classroom culture in which trying is seen as positive. Such a culture is discussed in the previous chapter.

In this scenario the groups actually need to be stopped. They need someone to help them to refocus on how they will learn to solve this puzzle. Words like: *think, listen to others, discuss, plan, decide, work together, try* and *don't give up* can all be explored through this initial phase of the activity.

Later when the task is completed these elements can be revisited with questions like:

What did you do?
How did you decide?
What learning skills did you need?
What would you do to make your solution better next time?

> How did you do as a group? What group skills did you need? How might you improve on these for another time?
>
> Can you think of any other situations where you might transfer this learning? Where else might you need these same skills for working together or in solving other problems?

This approach of setting a task in which pupils may have difficulty working out how to proceed is one that is rich in potential for providing an authentic context for a metacognitive discussion about *how* the pupils learn. The important thing here is that they struggle initially so that there is a purpose for applying skills such as *thinking, listening to others, discussing, planning, agreeing, working together, trying* and *not giving up*.

Thereafter each group could draw up a list of skills that they used during the task. This could be done by looking at an artefact, like a photograph or drawing, and discussing what they did, what they learned and how they learned it. It might be possible to annotate the artefact in some way, i.e. on a drawing or placing learning words around a photograph. Such items are useful to display in the classroom as reinforcement and reminders of how we learn and the language of learning.

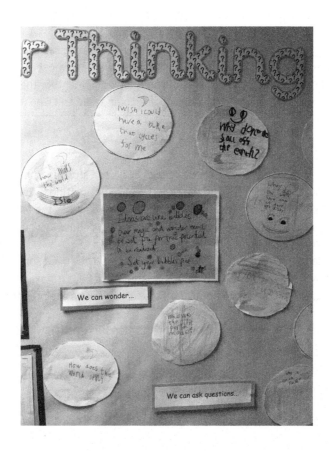

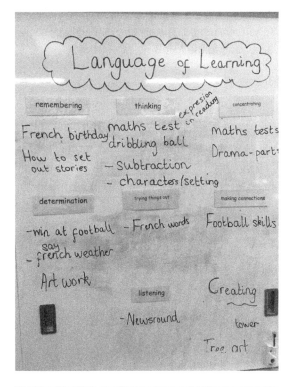

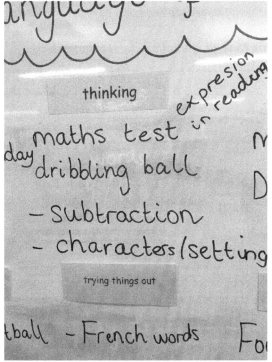

A next step in this consideration of the processes that they used to achieve the task might be one of reflection and self-evaluation. The group or individuals could look at the list of processes and sort them according to the following categories:

- We were great at these.
- We were okay at these.
- We need to work on these.

From this list, they can celebrate what they do well and set themselves a target for development. At the prompting of the teacher, they could look back at these identified strengths and targets before beginning a similar task.

Case Study 3: Newspaper technology

Resources

- sheets of newspaper rolled tightly into rods and taped – five or six per group (creating these can be part of the activity).

Learning intentions (including for metacognition)

- I can work as part of a team to solve a problem.
- I can apply my learning and skills to a problem.
- I can revise and improve my plans to make something work.
- I can explain what skills I have used and how I have solved a problem.

Metacognition focus (any of the following processes)

looking (observation)	listening	thinking
remembering	making connections	working collaboratively
guessing/predicting	trying out working out	improving – retrying

If the pupils are new to thinking about how they learn, it will be necessary for the teacher to use these words explicitly and draw the pupils' attention to them as they progress through the task. With a class who have more experience of the language of learning, there may be more emphasis on getting the pupils to identify the metacognition.

Activity

The task involves using newspaper rods. It will be necessary to begin by teaching the basic rolling technique before starting this activity. A pencil is used to begin the rolling of the newspaper sheet into a tightly rolled tube. This is taped to prevent it unrolling and then the pencil retrieved. Each group will need at least five newspaper rods each.

The task for each group is to use the newspaper rods to construct a bridge capable of supporting the weight of the teacher. (Or if you feel that this is pushing it too much, substitute something more appropriate from the classroom!) The groups are only allowed their newspaper rods and some extra tape.

Before the pupils begin the task they are told to revisit the skills they have discussed and developed in previous practical group tasks. They should share what they feel were their strengths and challenges. They should make sure that they are aware of their target skills to work on today.

They are given a fixed time to complete the task and are reminded to keep the skills they are using in mind as they go. There will be a learning skills list on the classroom wall for reference. At the end of the task there can be a plenary which enables the groups to discuss what they did, what they learned, and which skills they used or developed.

As the pupils work, the role of the teacher is to ask the kind of questions that will facilitate this kind of awareness:

Teacher:	What are you thinking about doing?
Pupil:	We could make like a frame out of the rolls of paper.
Teacher:	What does the task require?
Pupil:	Well it needs to be strong and I was thinking about the bridge I pass on the way to school.
Teacher:	What ideas do you have so far?
Pupil:	I think triangles might make it stronger.
Teacher:	What skills do you have to bring to this task?
Pupil:	When we worked before we all agreed to share our ideas before we began and then agree what to do. Then we had different jobs for everyone to do in the group.
Teacher:	How can you get the best out of your team?
Pupil:	We need to stop arguing and agree on a plan before we get going.

Metacognition

As in Case Study 2, it is sometimes better to allow a degree of trial and error and even disagreement in group activities before asking the pupils to stop and think. If you do this kind of activity often, the pupils will begin to realise that the best approach is not to rush in and do it, but instead to stop, think, discuss, agree, plan, etc.

The teacher can intervene or start the session with questions such as:

What skills will you bring to this task?
Why? What do you know that makes those appropriate skills?
How will you carry out the task?
What have you learned from our last lesson (crossing the swamp) that you can use here?
What are the skills of collaborative work?
What are you doing? Why? What is he/she doing?
Do you think that is a good idea? Why isn't it working?
How well do you think the group is cooperating?
Is there anything you might do differently/to improve this?

An approach to the plenary similar to that used in the last case study would again be appropriate. The pupils can list all the different skills that the group used on the task, record them on Post-it Notes and sort into the same three categories:

- We were great at these.
- We were okay at these.
- We need to work on these.

They can then be encouraged to celebrate any improvements in their learning skills and set a target for development.

Case Study 4: Poster challenge

Resources

- large poster paper and coloured pens for each group.

Learning intentions (including for metacognition)

The learning intentions for this activity could include some more subject-specific ones depending on the poster subject.

- I can demonstrate my understanding of ....
- I can work collaboratively as part of a group to achieve a task.
- I can share my opinions and listen to the opinions of others.
- I can explain what learning skills and approaches I have taken in my work.
- I can explain any transferable skills I have used.

Metacognition focus (any of the following processes)

working together	making decisions	cooperating
planning ahead	considering others	making improvements
making connections - linking thinking	using other knowledge	

Activity

The pupils have to work in groups to create a poster demonstrating all that they know about a given subject. For example, the subject could be a meaningful context such as Vikings at the end of a unit of such work or it could be based on something random, such as being a team player or the school grounds, in order to encourage thinking, negotiation and creativity.

The teacher specifies success criteria for the task. These may be determined by the theme and each group has to include these features/characteristics. For example, the poster should

- contain a combination of words and illustrations and at least one graph or table;
- give at least three facts;
- explain something clearly;

- be of more than one colour;
- not have any text or images borrowed from the internet.

Before the pupils begin the task they are told to identify the skills that they have used in previous practical group tasks. They should share what they feel were their strengths and challenges. They should make sure that they are aware of their target skills to work on today.

They are given a fixed time to complete the task and are reminded to keep the skills they are using in mind throughout. There will be a learning skills list on the classroom wall for reference.

Metacognition

At the end of the task the pupils will be asked, as before:

Reflect on what you did, why and how did you do it?
Look at the focus questions below and consider each one in turn.
Think of (and record) all the skills that you used in the task.
Sort these skills into three categories:

- We were great at these.
- We were okay at these.
- We need to work on these.

From this list celebrate any improvement in your learning skills.
And then set yourselves a target for development another time.

The reflection described in the box above is compatible with a process approach to almost any activity or task that might occur in or out of a primary school. What is important is the articulation of the learner's feelings and reflections about the learning and the development of their learning skills.

In order to achieve such reflection and articulation, the teacher has to model, articulate (through think alouds) and explore the pupils' developing understanding of learning and their developing learning skills. In this way the teacher can guide them to recognising the transferability of these skills to other areas of learning.

Case Study 5: Reading pictures

Resources

- large picturebook.

Learning intentions (including for metacognition)

The learning intentions for this activity are to learn about learning and to read a picture. This might be explored and expressed more specifically as:

- I can describe the learning skills I am using in this task.
- I can find information in a text/picture.

- I can make decisions about the text.
- I can justify my decisions with evidence.

Metacognition focus (any of the following processes)

looking	making connections	explaining and justifying thoughts
working out	using imagination	finding evidence

Activity

At the start of the lesson the teacher will ask the pupils to think about reading:

Teacher:	What learning skills do you need to read?
Pupil:	Looking, concentrating, making connections.
Pupil:	Thinking, considering, asking questions, using your imagination.

Pupils are asked to use a chart to plot any learning skills they use during the lesson. Next the teacher models how to look at a picture.

Teacher:	Tell me what you can see?
Pupil:	A boy in red shoes.
Teacher:	What else?
Pupil:	A tree with a face in it!
Teacher:	Well done, you *looked carefully* and you *made a connection* to something familiar.
Pupil:	I can see a basket in his hand and he's going into the woods.
Pupil:	Yes like Little Red Riding Hood - but it's a boy!
Teacher:	Well done, you have *explained* what you could see and provided *evidence* from the picture. You have also shown how you can make *connections* between what you can see and what you already know.
Teacher:	What else can you notice?
Pupil:	I can see a ... a shadow and it's a bit like Red Riding Hood!
Teacher:	Yes it does a bit doesn't it? Well done, you *looked carefully* and used your *imagination* to *work out* what you thought.

Having asked the questions and explicitly modelled the identification of the learning skills for the class, the next step is for the pupils to investigate a text/picture of their own. Each group is given a new picture to look at and they are challenged to annotate the picture to show what decisions they can make about it - for example what they can see, what do they think it means, and what evidence can they offer to support these decisions.

After a while the pupils are stopped for a meta-learning pit stop:

Teacher: Let's share something about how we are learning. Who can tell us which learning skills they have been using?

Once pupils have shared these they then share the product of their investigations of the text/picture. The role of the teacher here is to articulate *the way the pupils learned*: a focus on words such as yes you *looked*, you *used your imagination*, you made *connections*, etc. enables these skills to be more explicit and heightens the pupils' awareness of *how* they are learning.

Having identified the words that describe *how* they learned the teacher then asks:

In school:
Teacher: Where else in school do you use these skills?
Pupil: In music we have to *concentrate* and *read* the notes.
Pupil: In language we have to *read* the words and try to *understand* what they are saying.
Pupil: In topic work we have to *find information* and *provide evidence* about it.

Out of school:
Teacher: What about out of school? Where might you need these skills that you have been using today?
Pupil: When we play football we have to *listen* to the coach and *remember* our instructions.
Pupil: At Brownies we have to *look for clues* when we are playing wide games.
Pupil: On my computer game I need to *concentrate* and *find patterns* to get points.
Teacher: Yes, so you see that the skills we have been using today are useful not just for this reading task, but also for lots of other subjects where we learn in school. They are also useful out of school whether it is to do with school, sport or playing with your friends.

It is very important to identify these learning skills and make explicit the transferable nature of them. Helping pupils to realise that the skills have some relevance and use beyond school, in their own leisure activities, does help them to see that the skills are important for them - not just for the teacher!

How to learn better

This is the next step, and it might not be one to take at this point in the pupils' development. It is not enough simply to identify how we are learning. We need at some point to have a focus on each of these transferable learning skills and to try to develop and improve how we use them.

At the end of a lesson like this it might simply be enough to say:

> Choose one of these skills that you used today that you think you are good at.
> Tell your learning partner what that skill is and why you think you are good at it.
> Try to provide evidence to support what you say.

This self-assessment activity helps to consolidate the metacognition for the learners, not only the person telling their partner but also the person listening and asking questions.

At this point the teacher might go on to say:

> Choose one of these skills that you used today that you think you are not so good at.
> Tell your learning partner what that skill is and how you think you might get better at it. Try to provide evidence to support what you say.

This would be the beginning of the development stage where pupils think and talk about how to get better at their learning skills. Later on there might be whole class lessons of ways of being better at *remembering* or *finding evidence* or *looking* for a pattern.

However, the lesson itself might be step one. The self-assessment of the learning skills used might be step two. The identification of skills to focus on to develop together might be step three. It will all depend on the pupils, the teacher and the time available.

Key meta-learning focus questions

> What did you do?
> What was hard? Why?
> What was easy? Why?
> Which learning skills did you use?
> What do you learn about your own learning skills here?
> Which of these learning skills are a strength for you personally?
> Which of these learning skills do you need to work on to develop next?
> Where else might you use these skills?
> What did you do when you were stuck?
> How did you support each other?
> If you were doing an activity like this again what advice would you give yourself and your group?

Summary and key points

In this chapter we have highlighted the importance of the teacher's role in encouraging and supporting reflection and engaging the pupils in appropriate dialogue about learning. We explained the need for a focus on the language of learning and the need for the teacher to model, articulate and make explicit learning processes.

The case studies are designed with metacognition as their main focus. They give examples of ways that collaborative, class and individual learning tasks can be used to develop the pupils' ability to understand and talk about how they learn, and go on to use this knowledge in order to learn better. Case Study 5 explains how to develop awareness of transferable skills and identifies strategies for self-assessment.

Learning processes included in this chapter

Process	Case Study	Process	Case Study	Process	Case Study
looking (observation)	1, 3, 5	thinking	1, 2, 3	making connections	1, 3, 4, 5
guessing	1, 3	working out/trying out	1, 2, 3, 5	using other knowledge	1, 4
planning ahead	2, 4	cooperating, working together	2, 3, 4	making decisions	2, 4
remembering other learning	2, 3	listening	2, 3	making improvements: revisiting, revising, redrafting	2, 3, 4
considering others	4	solving problems	1	predicting	2
explaining thoughts and feelings	5	justifying suggestions and predictions	5	using imagination	5
looking for patterns	5	finding evidence	5		

Next steps for the reader

- Consider how you might introduce the concept of metacognition to your class. Where are they in this process? Are they new to metacognition or will you be building on prior awareness?
- Try out some of the case studies as appropriate.
- Does your class have a shared understanding of the language of learning words?
- Look at your existing plans: identify how the pupils will be learning, how they will achieve the learning intentions. This is not *what* they do, but *how*; the skills they will need.

9 A whole school approach

Any teacher can introduce a metacognitive approach into their teaching. However, there is great benefit to having a whole school approach in which there is a focus on *how* we learn and the language of learning throughout the school. This chapter considers how to implement a whole school approach, starting with the need to give teachers the knowledge, skills and understanding required in order to adopt such an approach. We explain how to use whole school CPD to encourage everyone to reflect on *how* they learn and *how* the children learn. School assemblies are explored as a means of developing not only the language of learning but a shared understanding of learning and also of what specific learning processes might look like across the school.

Introduction

Like any educational development or initiative it would be easy to go in for a big impact launch with INSET meetings and resources and lots of enthusiasm, only to find that this is not sustainable in the long term. As with any educational initiative, success will only come if those involved are on board and fully understand the *what*, the *why* and the *how* of the approach. In this chapter we will explore some ways this can be done.

How to implement a whole school approach

In order to establish a whole school approach towards developing metacognition it may be necessary to devote some CPD or INSET time to sharing and developing a communal understanding. What are we looking for? What kind of learning processes are we targeting? Do we all mean the same thing by the terms we use? What are our expectations of a metacognitive approach? Why are we establishing a metacognitive approach?

A good way to start is by asking the key question: What makes a good learner? If you ask the pupils this question, their answers will be something like this:

- listens well;
- sits quietly;

- has neat writing;
- sits still;
- keeps their hands and feet to themselves;
- doesn't shout out;
- works hard;
- well behaved;
- gets everything right.

If you ask parents, they might respond might like this:

- a good listener;
- well behaved;
- patient;
- wants to learn about topics;
- listens well;
- does his best;
- tries hard even if you don't get it right;
- does as he's told;
- asks questions;
- puts her hand up;
- doesn't shout out;
- values learning;
- does well.

At an INSET it is useful to begin by asking the teachers what makes a good learner. Their responses can be compared to the responses from pupils and parents. Is there agreement amongst the staff team or are there striking differences of opinion?

What is interesting is the focus on behaviour. Most people think, initially, about a good learner as someone who has good learning *behaviour*. The first things that come to mind are things like: sits quietly, puts her hand up, behaves well, etc.

However, we need to shift the focus from *learning behaviour* as a social interaction to the *behaviour of learning* in a skill sense.

This involves some specific learning skills and dispositions. Things like being determined, showing resilience, working in a team, negotiating, remembering, working things out, trying different methods, looking for a pattern, etc.

What makes a good learner?

The first INSET activity, then, might be a mindmap or carousel that considers what makes a good learner. The next step would be to guide the discussion away from learning behaviour towards learning skills and dispositions.

One possible way to do this is to get the staff to draw up a mindmap, listing skills and atti-tudes towards learning that are *transferable*. The important thing here is that those involved need to go beyond task and subject-specific skills such as know your tables, is a good speller and is well-organised, to transferable skills such as remembering, applying strategies and organising tasks logically.

Once the staff team have agreed what the transferable skills might be called, there is a need to develop strategies for making these skills and the associated vocabulary much more explicit throughout all teaching. Instead of praising a pupil for sitting quietly, teachers should be saying 'Well done, Susan, you were listening and thinking and learning'.

As a staff it is important to develop a shared understanding of the kind of language to model and encourage in class with regard to learning about learning. Whole school CPD needs to encourage everyone to reflect on *how* they learn and *how* the children learn.

The language of learning

Having identified that there is a difference between *what* we learn and *how* we learn, and between classroom behaviour and *learning* behaviour, it is important to explore ways of developing the kind of ethos and language that will support this development in the classroom.

Staff need to consider how the learners will be able to talk about their learning and to develop ways of articulating how they learn before they can think meaningfully about how they might work on *getting better* at their learning. Elsewhere in this book we have looked at how to introduce this with pupils. At an INSET it is very valuable to go through these activities with the staff so that everyone has a shared understanding of the importance of exploring and developing an understanding of the language of learning in their classrooms.

One of the aims of a metacognitive approach is that children think about these words for learning and their transferable learning skills. As explained above, it is important when introducing staff to this approach that there is some focus on the learning processes and transferable skills. Getting teachers to think about the list of skills and dispositions and to share where they have used them both *in* and *out* of school is a good way to make this learning more explicit.

For example, a teacher might say that she has to be able *to problem solve*, *explain carefully* and *concentrate* in order to be successful in her teaching. These skills are also important beyond school, for example in juggling the organisation and management of a family these organisational skills will be very useful! Similarly, if a teacher says that she enjoys DIY and gardening at home we might probe a little to ascertain that learning skills and dispositions like *planning*, *creativity*, *trial and error*, and *resilience* all feature in these pastimes. All of these skills and dispositions transfer readily to learning in education. If we can help the staff to understand these transferable connections it will be easier for them to make these more explicit when working on metacognition with their pupils in school.

It is also important for the person leading the INSET to use consistently the language of learning that has been discussed throughout this book. Some of the examples in Chapters 5, 6, 7 and 8 might be useful as models of metacognition and of profiling the language of learning.

At the end of the INSET the staff team should understand what is meant by a metacognitive approach, what language and learning processes they are targeting and how to begin to put the approach into action. Once staff understand and are committed to adopting this approach, it is important to support them in taking things forward. There are suggestions, strategies and examples throughout this book that will support and structure the introduction of metacognition in the classroom.

Whole school approaches

Planning

In addition, it might be useful to end the INSET with discussion about how metacognition can be made more a part of everyday classroom practice. For example, there could be some discussion about how to include it in planning. It might be agreed that as well as specifying metacognition in the learning intentions at the start of a lesson, there will be a focus on one or two of the words from the language of learning list.

For example, in a literacy lesson you might have:

Learning intention

We are learning to create a story which will have some emotional impact on the reader.

Learning skill

We are learning to *share* ideas and to *reflect* on our work and give useful *feedback* to others.

Success criteria

I can use WOW words to have impact on the reader.
I can structure my story with

- an arresting opening;
- a turning point for dramatic effect;
- an unusual ending.

Assembly

It is important to encourage a permeation of this approach throughout the school and weekly assemblies or gatherings are an ideal opportunity for doing so. In one school we visited they hold what they call a Citizenship Assembly once a week. This provides an ideal opportunity for the development of ethos, values and, of course, for sharing a collective understanding of some of the language of learning. Each week, one or more words were profiled (see Appendix 3 'Resources for Profiling the Language' for examples).

These gatherings provide a forum for developing a focus on the topic of *how* to learn. They are also an opportunity to show how these learning skills might look at different ages and stages in the school, from the youngest interpretations of *choosing* or *remembering* to the oldest. Although there will be a lot of difference, there will also be much that is similar.

Assemblies are also a good opportunity to celebrate successes. Collectively pupils can be asked:

Who has done some *remembering* this week?
How did you go about it?
Does anyone else have a different strategy?
How did *remembering* help you to learn?

Walk through

Members of the management team can follow up such assemblies and go round the classes asking the pupils follow-up questions. This would send out a clear signal of the value placed on this initiative. It would also provide the management team with some evidence of the assemblies' impact.

Even if words are not profiled in assembly it is still a good idea for the management team to take opportunities to interact with pupils, incidentally, about how they are learning. It might simply be by asking that 'how' question:

Adult:	Tell me what you are doing just now.
Learner:	I am drawing a picture of a castle.
Adult:	And what are you learning?
Learner:	I'm learning to draw and I am learning about the different bits of a castle from this book.
Adult:	And *how* are you learning?

With experience, the child might be able to answer with something like:

I have to *look* carefully. I am copying the parts onto my drawing.
I need to *remember* to draw without pressing hard so that my sketch lines can be erased later.

In order to support this the teacher might take up the role of articulating the sub-skills that are being used. In particular, they should focus on skills that are transferable, such as those listed in the example above.

Well done. You *looked* carefully and made an accurate drawing of the castle.
By *looking* carefully you have found out more about the design of the castle.
You have *remembered* what you learnt in art about sketching. This has helped you make a good representation of the castle.

Whole school displays

It might be useful to set up a communal metacognition board or display where pupils are reminded of the language of learning. Ideally such a display might have the capacity for pupils to add something about their metacognitive experiences to share with others. A display can be made interactive, for example, by having a pad of Post-its available so that pupils can record examples of when they have been doing something profiled such as *sharing* or *organising information*. This in turn becomes part of the display and provides examples (and evidence) of how the learning skill is being used in school.

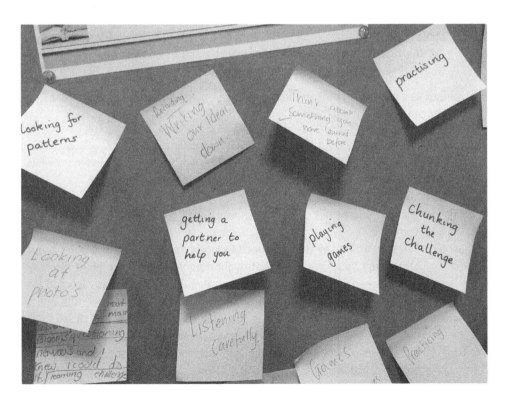

In celebrations

Staff can be encouraged to use the language of learning as much as possible and to make the learning skills explicit. When praising pupils or giving out certificates the focus could be on *how* you learned, rather than on *what* you learned. In this way a whole school ethos can be established and developed.

Creating school characters

It might be helpful for each class in the school to have a conversation about some of the words/skills. They could be set the task of producing a poster to advertise/explain a particular skill. They could even have characters to represent different skills and dispositions, e.g. Danny Determined, Ruby Remember, Terry Try Hard.

A development of this idea is to have a whole school or whole class character to represent what a really good learner looks like, in terms of how they might think, act and respond to learning challenges. There is a description of such a lesson in Chapter 7, which focuses on the middle years.

Case Study 1: Lexi the Learner

1   Do the activity: 'Learning carousel: What makes a good learner?' (see Appendix 1.7).
2   Filter results to exclude behaviour descriptors.
3   Create a class version of the perfect learner:

- Draw around a child and call the character something unisex like Lexi Learner (see photos opposite).
- Get the class to write words around this character to reflect how a good learner would think (inside the frame) and act (outside).

4   Use Lexi as a reference point so that when children are embarking on a task the teacher can say things such as:

Teacher:	Today we are looking at some new spelling words. Now who can tell me what Lexi might be thinking when faced with a remembering task?
Child:	Look carefully.
Child:	Listen.
Child:	Think.
Teacher:	Yes, Lexi would say that you need to *look carefully*, *listen* and *think* about other work you have done that might help you here. Lexi might also say that we need to go over some of the *strategies* we have already learned for *working things out*, and for *remembering*.
Teacher:	Oh you are stuck? Well, what do you think Lexi would do in this situation? Lexi would tell you to *look carefully* at what you were asked to do. Lexi might also say *think* about where you might have come across something like this before. Words like *don't give up* and *resilience* might be used, don't you think?

Determined: Dazi is a kind and friendly mouse, she tells us not to give up. She sets a target and then breaks it into smaller targets to reach her goal. Try different strategies to have success.

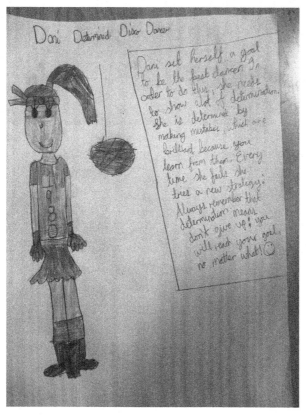

Dani Determined Disco Dancer

Dani set herself a goal to be the best dancer. In order to do this, she needs to show a lot of determination. She is determined by making mistakes, which are brilliant because you learn from them. Every time she fails she tries a new strategy. Always remember that determination means don't give up; you will reach your goal, no matter what! ☺

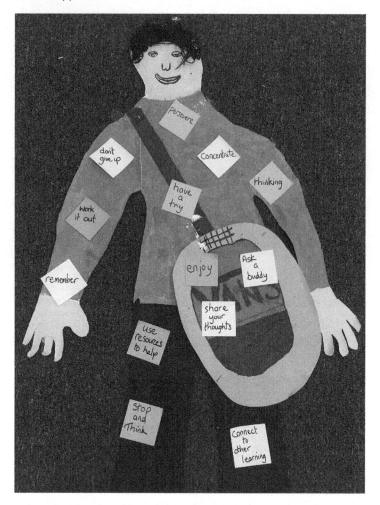

5   Have some way of making visible the *way* they are learning, for example:

- There might be an exit pass for a lesson where pupils write on Post-its two words to describe how they have been learning.
- Each child might have a sheet with learning words on it to colour in or tally each time they think they have been using one of the skills (see Appendix 5.1).
- There might be a plenary or learning conversation where the way they have been learning is articulated and made explicit.

6   Once a culture of reflecting on how we learn has been established in the class, the next step is to discuss ways to improve so that the focus moves on to how we learn *best*.

Transferable learning

In order to establish that teachers are in the business of enabling pupils to learn skills and strategies that will help them to learn beyond school and throughout their lives, it is important to stress the transferability of learning skills and the awareness of how we learn best.

Thinking about how we learned before we came to school

One way to do this is to take opportunities to reflect on how the learning skills are applicable before school, in school and beyond school. For example, when discussing learning you might explore:

Teacher:	Think back to a time before you ever came to school. What kind of things did you learn to do?
Child:	I learned to talk, and to walk.
Child:	I learned to ride my bike.
Child:	I learned to swim, do cartwheels.
Teacher:	How did you learn to walk? To swim? To talk? To eat?
	Did you need to put up your hand, sit nicely, have your hands in a basket, get on with others?
	No, well what did you do then? What skills did you need?
Children:	To listen, to copy, to try hard, to do a bit at a time.

This helps the children to identify the transferable learning skills and dispositions that make a good learner. They can also have conversations about things they are currently learning, beyond school, for example:

Teacher:	What kind of learning do you do out of school?
Children:	Judo, football training, violin, mountain biking.
Teacher:	So what skills do you need for this learning?
	(Various responses are likely here.)
Teacher:	So, can you think of any of these skills that you use after school that might help you when you are in school?

We can also make explicit how the things they do in school might transfer across subject boundaries and even beyond school. For example, we might ask them about a skill and then get them to list experiences where they might use this skill. Below is an example of how this was done in class using a learning carousel approach to explore the word 'persevering'. The pupils were asked to think and talk about situations when they had to persevere in school and out of school, and to consider what persevering actually looks, feels and sounds like. (See Appendix 1.7 for details of the learning carousel approach.)

Reflecting on how we learn

It might be beneficial to have a whole school approach to reflection on how we learn. This could be done in a number of ways.

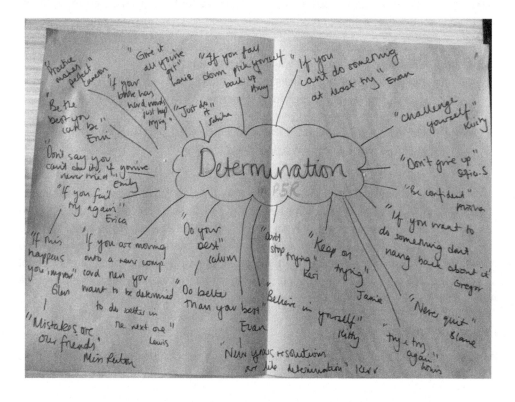

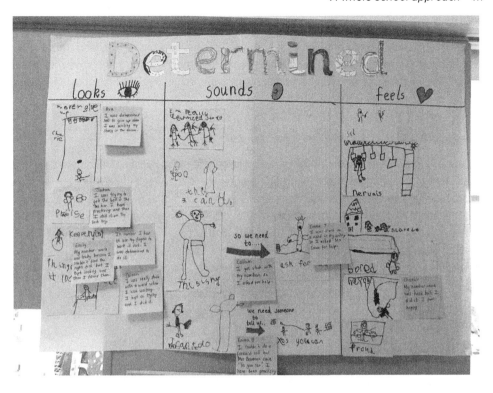

Learning conversations

Put simply, this can mean any conversation with a focus on *how* we are learning. It should lead into consideration of *ways* in which we learn and then lead on to how we might learn *better*. These conversations can be formal or informal, structured or unstructured. It is best to do this kind of thing little and often.

Artefacts as a focus for learning discussions

For discussions about how we are learning it might sometimes be valuable to have some sort of artefact to focus upon. There might be an agreement that each class will focus on learning in, for example, art. Pupils might take out a picture or model they have been working on and talk about the kind of learning skills they had to use and develop whilst engaged in the task. The teacher will need to guide their language of learning and try to steer them towards thinking about the more transferable skills that were involved.

Teachers/peers might ask:

> What skills did you need to use here?
> Which skills were easy for you?
> Which were more difficult?
> Where else have you used these skills? In school? Out of school?
> What other skills might you have used instead?
> What might you do to become better at these skills?
> What can you do to get better?
> Who can help you?
> How can you help yourself?

The aim here is to involve the pupils as much as possible so that they see learning as something that they own, that they have much more control over than they might think. It should be impressed upon them that learning doesn't *happen to* them, but that *they make it happen*.

A timetabled slot

Whilst it is easy to see the benefits of thinking and talking about how we learn, it is sometimes too easy to get so involved in learning and teaching that not enough attention is given to reflecting on how we learn. Therefore it might be helpful to have a whole school decision to timetable in a reflection time where such conversations can take place.

Discussion linked to PLPs

If your school has some kind of personal learning plans (PLPs) for the children it might be a good idea to link these to the language of learning and the metacognition about how we learn. Certainly there should be some evidence in the kind of reflections and targets about learning that is recorded in these documents. Hopefully you might come to see less of the 'I want to get better at my tables' and more of the 'I am going to try some different strategies for remembering my tables'.

As part of the plenary at the end of a lesson/day

It could be that you decide, as a school, that you will end some lessons with a brief focus on the way the class have been learning. It is probably best, however, if this isn't done for every lesson, every day. Such overkill would dilute the benefit of this approach. Having a 15-minute slot at the end of most days to look back at what they have learned and how they have learned would be a better approach.

During lessons

As mentioned elsewhere in this book, it may be useful to have occasional reflective pit stops where the teacher can draw attention to the transferable skills being used and developed during a lesson.

Peer learning interactions

As described in Chapter 4, a peer learning approach requires the children to have some training in the skills of facilitating for a peer who is reflecting on their learning. With some scaffolding, and perhaps a set of generic questions to work from, pupils can work together with one person prompting another to reflect and articulate how they have been learning and how they might go on to learn *better*.

Periodic displays and events

For example:

- each class can make a poster;
- one class does an assembly;
- develop a whole school interactive display;
- use Post-it activities;
- teachers can nominate a learner of the week.

Activities linked to or devised by the pupil council or learning council

See below for discussion on this.

Working together

Where possible, it is important to involve the children in having responsibility for the work on learning discussions. For example:

Learning partners

As mentioned above, it is beneficial for pupils to work together to talk about how they learn. Learning conversations and peer learning interactions are ways to do this.

Learning buddies

It may be possible to partner up older pupils with younger ones so that the older learning buddies can support and scaffold the younger ones to think and talk about how they learn. The older children benefit from these conversations as they can be a reminder of the steps towards learning and of some of the learning skills that may now be so implicit they are no longer aware of them.

Learning council

The school might have pupils who represent each class in a weekly gathering as a learning council. Part of their remit might be to share, develop and promote the language of learning. They might plan assemblies and whole school initiatives and celebrations. They might be the ones to select the word of the week when the teachers are exploring some of the learning skills and strategies with their classes. They could be involved in information sessions for parents on the metacognitive approach (see below).

Parental involvement

It is important to include the parents in the development of a metacognitive approach. A session for parents, similar to the one for teachers and pupils, where they explore what makes a good learner might be a good place to begin. Communication is also important and words being explored at school can be shared with parents via the pupils' homework tasks, through the school website and via Twitter. Parents can be encouraged to share and celebrate success in terms of *how* their child learns, instead of in terms of what they achieve. Instead of 'My son learned how to pitch a tent this weekend', a parent might say 'My son learned how to cooperate, follow instructions and persevere when camping this weekend'.

In one school where this ethos had been introduced, the feedback from parents suggested that:

> At the curriculum evening the parents really liked that the children were talking about their learning and about *how* they were learning. They said that they felt this would help them to be better able to support their children with their learning. There was positive feedback from the parents.

Beyond the school

Apart from the involvement within the school and the involvement of parents it is beneficial to involve other schools and agencies. In our recent work with a group of primary schools we saw the benefits of an Associated Schools Group (ASG) focus on how we learn. (An ASG is a coordinated cluster of local primary schools working towards common goals.) It was possible to deliver INSET to introduce and explore the language of learning with staff. Those involved went on to try things out in their own schools. Later they brought pupils from their learning councils to have some input into the training event. Again the cascading approach was beneficial, with the children going back to their schools, each determined to try to promote the language of learning and a metacognitive awareness with their peers. There was also a meeting where each of the pupil councils from the different schools in the group met to share the things they had been doing in their own schools and to plan other things that they might be do next.

This concerted and coordinated approach meant that the pupils moving on to the same high school had already had a shared experience in addition to a shared understanding of a learning vocabulary. Clearly the next step would be to work with staff at high schools so that such initiatives do not get left in the primary school.

Summary approach to introduce metacognition as a whole school initiative

Below is an outline of some of the stepping stones to introducing the metacognition approach in school.

Note that this process is not strictly linear. Children will move through stages in irregular timing, for example they may still be working on the language of learning whilst also using knowledge about themselves as learners in order to learn better. All stages are essential but some overlap.

Language of learning – introduce and embed (see Chapter 2)	
Reflect on what makes a good learner • with staff on INSET; • with pupils in their classes; • with parents, if possible.	Establish the difference between • learning behaviour; and • learning skills and dispositions.
Reflect on self as a learner: • How do I learn? What skills do I use? • Do I transfer these skills/attitudes etc. from one curricula area to another, from school to home, from when I was much younger to now.	
Have learning conversations where we share our developing understanding of how we learn – thinking and talking about learning.	Begin to plan for *how* we learn as well as *what* we learn – the teacher planning and the child thinking ahead to their work.
Metacognition – find ways of illustrating *when* and *how* these learning skills are being used.	Think of ways of using knowledge about learning skills and self as a learner to learn better.
Employ whole school approaches to reinforce and value work done in the classrooms, such as • having a weekly focus on one of the learning skill/dispositions; • celebrating examples of good practice – innovative ways to be metacognitive; • sharing with parents the information about metacognition, e.g. send the word of the week home, share the poster X did, showing how he was challenged this week and how he overcame that challenge; • encouraging staff to talk more about how we learn than what we learn – culture in staffroom and classroom.	

Language of learning - introduce and embed (see Chapter 2)
Make the integration of metacognition into planning a formal part of the planning process and planning format.
Look for evidence around the school of • metacognitive talk, e.g. there might be a timetabled slot for peer learning conversations; • learner identity and becoming better at the skills of learning.
Pupils are encouraged to play an active role in metacognition by • flagging it up; • talking about learning; • talking about how to make it better; • being responsible for developing their own metacognition; • through demonstrating their awareness in posters, presentations and displays.

Summary and key points

In this chapter we considered ways of introducing and developing a focus on how we learn as a whole school approach. We looked at activities that could be used in an INSET day with the whole staff, ways in which to involve parents and, most importantly, we looked at how we could give a sense of ownership to the pupils themselves.

We considered opportunities in and around school, such as assemblies, displays and class-room talk, as well as work with learning partners and a range of ideas to structure reflection on how we learn.

Next steps for the reader

Whether you read this chapter as a leader of learning in your school or as a class teacher interested in developing this approach, there should be things that you might do in your context. There is a whole raft of ideas in the chapter, and indeed in the whole book to get you started. One note of caution, however, it is better to do little and often than have a huge launch that is difficult to sustain once the novelty wears off!

The route to success is to make slight changes that are sustainable and, wherever possible, empower the pupils themselves to lead and manage ways of reflecting on how they learn, and how they learn *best*.

10 Becoming better learners

This chapter explores how to use knowledge about learning to become better at learning. It explores how, as learners become more aware of how they learn and the many different skills they employ to achieve a task, this knowledge can be used to help future learning. Value is placed on an environment in which many different approaches are encouraged. There is lengthy consideration of how to evaluate progress: how effective is the metacognitive approach and what impact is this having on the children? The chapter concludes with acknowledgement of the importance of sustaining the approach and how to celebrate success.

Introduction

Much of this book has explored the many ways of developing metacognition in the classroom so that learners understand *how* they learn. Developing the language of learning, trying different ways of learning and having learning conversations are all ways of promoting this learning awareness. However, if we want to help children to understand *how they learn best* we need to consider how to support and assess the impact of these metacognitive strategies on their overall learning. We also need to consider how this understanding about *how* we learn can inform our actions and attitudes towards learning *better*.

Becoming better learners

How does having the language of learning, being able to identify the processes pupils use and having increased awareness of how they learn help children to learn better?

Once pupils have some understanding about the importance of the actual skills involved in learning and know how these provide the basis for *all learning*, they can begin to focus on developing strategies and processes that help them to learn *best*. A climate and ethos in the classroom or school needs to acknowledge and promote the idea that we are all different and there does not have to be only one way of doing the learning. There needs to be a culture of experimenting and discussing learning approaches. Learners need to have more focus on *how* they learn and be encouraged to be brave and to try new approaches in the quest for the way that they can learn best. One way to encourage this is to have some focus on transferable learning skills and on learning dispositions.

This whole process is about enabling the learners to take more responsibility for *how* they learn. It is about providing alternative approaches and strategies so that the learner can approach a challenge from different angles. This means that they are less likely to stumble when they encounter something new or overly challenging. This greater ownership of learning that can come from this increased responsibility for, and awareness of, how they learn is one of the benefits to pupils identified in Chapter 1, where some of the research and theory underpinning this metacognitive approach is considered.

There's more than one way to be right!

As a part of general classroom practice there should be scope to ask the learners what learning approaches they used to achieve a task and to learn more. This then allows for acknowledgement and celebration of multiple approaches. Indeed, if pupils can offer different strategies to share, the teacher can utilise the opportunity to encourage all the pupils to experiment with a strategy they have never tried before. The ethos should be, *let's try this another way and see which approach suits me best*. For example, this is quite common practice in some maths classrooms:

The children have been given a word problem to solve individually. They then come together as a group to discuss their work.

Teacher: I don't want to know what answers you have yet. I want to hear how you tackled the problem.

Child: There are 8 schools with 97 children so I knew that the total number of children at the concert had to be 8 lots of 97.

Teacher: You have *thought* about the problem and *worked out* a way to solve it. Does everyone agree with that first step? Is that the sum needed to solve the problem?

(General consensus from class.)

Teacher: So, once you worked out how to do the problem, how did you work out the answer?

Child: I knew that 97 is near 100 so I worked out what 8 lots of 100 would be, and then I took away 8 lots of 3 because 97 is 3 less than 100.

Teacher: That sounds like a good strategy. You *thought* carefully, *remembered* some number facts and used those to help you work out a way forward. Did anyone do this in a different way?

Child: Yes. I am not very good at tables but I am good at adding, so I put 97 down 8 times and I added them all together.

Teacher: You used what you know about your own skills and approached this in the best way for you. Well done.

Child: I did 8 times 90 and then 8 times 7. I had to use paper to work it out.

Teacher:	Why did you use paper?
Child:	I needed to see the numbers and do the multiplication in the way you showed us.
Teacher:	Excellent. You used what you know about your own learning. You *remembered* and used a strategy you had been taught before.
Teacher:	Okay. Hold up your answers. All round the classroom, you used different ways to solve the same problem and you came up with the same answer. Well done. What does this tell you about learning in maths?
Child:	There's lots of different ways.
Child:	We should do it our own way.

This helps create a culture in which it is safe to experiment with ways to learn and to share individual approaches. Such a culture helps to foster a real sense of an effective learning community.

Of course there is a curriculum to be delivered and there are many things that need to be taught. Different pressures on the teacher will always be pushing towards attainment and tangible progress for the learners. Nevertheless it is still possible, even within the most goal-orientated and prescriptive curriculum, to stop for a moment and explore our thinking, to share our approaches, and to encourage our learners to see if doing things a different way will help them to learn better. The reflective pit stops mentioned earlier in the book might be a way to embed this in daily classroom practice.

It is the intention of this book to demonstrate how this metacognitive approach can be utilised, even when time is short and pressure is high.

A culture of joint endeavour

If the aim of this book is to help children understand *how they learn best* we need to acknowledge that it is something that cannot be done alone. We have explored how the teachers and other adults can model their own learning approaches, through think alouds, by using the language of learning and by scaffolding the learning conversations. We have considered how we can develop a better understanding of the skills that are required to be a successful learner. Next we need to focus on the notion that *how to learn* is a vast area to be explored, and doing this successfully is only possible as a joint endeavour.

In the past, learning was seen as something fairly transmissive: the learner soaking up wisdom from the sage. It was seen as something to be done independently and, often, in complete silence. There are many learning theories, however, that see learning as something socially constructed; it needs some communication and interaction. Moreover, educators need to move towards learning as something less fixed and more experimental. Instead of the teacher telling the pupils what to do and how to do it, modern classrooms have more of an enquiry approach. The child becomes increasingly responsible for their learning, with greater ownership and independence, while the teacher facilitates this more individual learning process. Many classrooms use a series of challenges where groups need to work out for themselves what to do and how to do it. This allows for the building of lifelong skills, attitudes and capacities. This kind of critical thinking provides an important opportunity to explore, share and develop different ways of learning. The following activity can be a good way to scaffold the process from directed learning to such independent approaches.

Activity: Origami rabbit

The children are told that they must make an origami rabbit. Each group is given paper and directed to complete the task in a specific way:

- Group 1 is given paper and told to get on with it, with no further input.
- Group 2 is given a page of written step-by-step instructions (no pictures) and paper.
- Group 3 is given paper and told to listen to step-by-step instructions.
- Group 4 is given an origami rabbit and paper to recreate another.
- Group 5 is given a series of photographs of an origami rabbit being constructed.

The children are given time to complete the task and then return as a whole group to discuss their experience. Each group needs to explain how they were asked to work. The focus in this learning discussion is on the different ways they were told to carry out the task. This could be facilitated with questions such as:

> Did you manage to make a rabbit?
> What was difficult about the way you carried out the task?
> What was easy?
> Can you see what was different about the approaches?
> If you could choose which way to make the rabbit, which way would it be?
> Why?
> Would you have found a different way harder?
> Why?
> Could we have combined some of the approaches to make an even better way to learn how to make the rabbit?

The outcome of the activity and discussion should be a heightened awareness that there are multiple ways to achieve a task, and that some people will find some approaches suit them better than others. There is not necessarily a best way to learn; rather there may be a way that suits an individual better.

Transferable learning skills and learning dispositions

Many schools are exploring learning dispositions with their pupils. Having a focus for the classroom or for the whole school enables a spotlight to be put on some of the attitudes and approaches towards learning. The work on mindset from Dweck (2012) and on visible learning from Hattie (2011) have influenced many schools to begin to make learners much more aware of how they go about their learning. In many countries, curriculum changes have encouraged pupils to take on much more responsibility for their own learning. All of this adds up to a signpost that stresses the significance of transferable learning skills. There is so much to learn nowadays that we cannot hope to learn it all. However, teachers do need to equip learners with the skills to approach all of their learning with confidence. What children need is to know how to learn and how they learn best in a variety of different contexts. The approaches outlined in this book, where we ask the learners to think about where their learning is successful, inside or outside of school, and to use the skills involved to support their other learning, shows how to encourage and build learning for life.

Once pupils begin to think about the processes that they use to learn, they can also become aware of the attitudes that have facilitated these processes. One approach towards recognising the importance of attitude in learning is to explore a word like *determined*. The pupils can consider what being determined looks like, feels like and sounds like. They can also identify learning processes such as *trying out*, *revising* and *improving* that would benefit from being approached with a determined attitude.

The class can then use this heightened awareness of what it is to be determined in order to set individual goals to strive for. Alternatively, they could create an advice mindmap where they make *determined* statements to motivate each other. They should be encouraged to make the link between the attitude and the learning. For example:

I managed to remember and use other learning because I was determined to solve the problem.

I listened to what the others in my group had to say because I was determined to be a good member of the team.

Such an approach could be used for any of the learning dispositions in order to illustrate the transferable aspects of learning how to learn best.

Assessing progress

It is important to consider what you are looking for when you are assessing progress. It might be useful for the class teacher to start by reflecting on what they think the progress will look like.

Some of the teachers we have been working with found that the change in language was what they noticed first. The children began using the language of learning. They also soon became more honest about their learning because they had the confidence to express fears and pride within the supportive ethos that accompanied the introduction of a metacognitive approach. One teacher found that he also became more honest about his teaching, admitting to his class that an approach he had used had not worked very well and that it would be better if he tried another way. This in turn helped raise awareness of the many approaches possible and served as a reminder that there is no shame in admitting when you get something wrong, but in fact it can be something that you can learn from.

Reflections from teachers after initial work to embed a metacognitive approach included the following:

- The more they do it [talk about their learning] the easier it is for them to do.
- I think it is important the whole school is doing this.

- It would be nice for the children to already have the foundation of the words. A lot of time has been spent understanding the words. Now they know them we can do more things to help the children think about their learning.

Developing a metacognitive approach is a stepped process as well as an iterative one. The kind of progress to be assessed should reflect the steps taken along the way. It might be helpful to ask questions like:

- Do the children have a passive understanding of the language of learning?
- Are the children using the language of learning appropriately during reflective sessions?
- Is there evidence that the children understand the language of learning that they are using?
- Are the children engaging in thinking and talking about their learning even when not prompted to?
- Is thinking and talking about learning becoming part of their daily practice?
- Are the children using knowledge about how they learn to make decisions about learning?
- Are the children using knowledge about how they learn to overcome challenges and learn better?
- Is attainment rising?
- Is there evidence that children have more confidence as learners?

Clearly it is easier to compare progress if you have the foresight to take a snapshot before you take your first steps down the path to metacognition. It might be useful to do an audit for the class or whole school where you find out just how well the pupils understand how they go about their learning. This can take many different forms:

Pupil questionnaires

Pupils might be asked some questions about *how* they learn, what do they do when they get stuck, what is their attitude towards *not* succeeding with their learning, and what is their attitude towards trying new approaches. A sample questionnaire can be found in Appendix 1.2.

The questionnaires might help the teacher determine what the children need and the best way to begin to introduce a metacognitive approach. This information can then be revisited. A repeat questionnaire after the metacognitive ideas from this book have had time to embed in the school may reveal a difference of attitude. Children should begin to have different responses to questions about what to do when they are stuck and about how they learn, and they may have different attitudes towards making mistakes. This is the first stage in a long-term process. As this initiative is more about opening minds, shifting attitudes and developing approaches to learning, it may be some time before it is possible to see the impact of the approach on attainment.

When we trialled this approach in schools the initial questionnaire before the approach was introduced produced responses such as the following:

> I don't like it if the work is hard. I don't know what to do and I feel bad.

Yet, after a few months of some work on the language of learning the responses demonstrated some shift in attitudes:

> You learn more if it is something harder. If it is fun but a bit trickier, you finally get the answer after trying lots of times, you learn it better, remember it more because you had so many tries to get it right.

Interviews

You may want to hold some interviews with a range of learners. Again you would focus on asking them to talk about their recent learning and their attitude towards it. Such interviews can be recorded or transcribed so that you can make comparisons at some point in the future. This is also valuable as a means of showing parents, school boards, etc. what you are trying to achieve and how well you are progressing. In particular, the development of the language of learning is quite apparent if you host the interviews before and after a whole school drive to raise awareness and use of the words that describe *how* we learn.

The extracts below are from an interview with four children in an upper primary class towards the end of the first year of using a metacognitive approach.

> *How do you learn best?*
>
> I learn by asking questions.
>
> I learn well by reading books. I enjoy reading. Mum often asks me where did you find that out and I say, I read a book.
>
> When you talk about your learning it makes you remember it even more.
>
> Visually – by seeing the thing – going to see it and then coming back and finding out more, with the picture of it in my head to help me remember my learning ...
>
> *Can you say a bit more about what you mean?*
>
> I remember we were doing maths. The teacher wrote the question on the board, we could all see it and we could tell her the answer, but when she doesn't write it on the board I can't remember it and then I can't tell her the answer. I like writing the question down in maths. It just falls out if I try to keep it in my head.
>
> *What makes you know you are good at learning?*
>
> There's something inside me that says I'm not very good at maths. Your brain tells you if you have got the answer or if you are struggling you know I am not very good at this.
>
> *What helps you to learn?*
>
> We have a times table chart and if you are struggling you can look at it.

We have spelling patterns on the wall and you can look them up if you get stuck.

I try it out on a piece of paper and if it looks right I use it and if it doesn't I look on the wall.

It comes back to enjoyment because if you enjoy what you are doing you'll want to try hard and you'll want to do more, but if you don't enjoy it, you'll avoid it.

I like it when there's a good atmosphere in the classroom. It just feels good and we feel like getting on with our work.

Sometimes you think, why am I learning this? Is it important and you think not really, but other times you realise it is important so you think I must try a bit harder.

It depends on how determined you are to get it right. You'll think I'll need this in later life. Sometimes you think I'll not try that hard because I don't think I'll need this in later life. I'm not fussed.

But sometimes the teacher just hasn't explained that. We were doing decimals and everyone was saying, why do I need to know this? What's the point? Then Miss Green explained about when you're running, a point in the middle can change a number completely from it being 300 to 3.00 and that makes a big difference in runners' times. We were making things in art and we realised it was maths. If we hadn't learned how to make circles with a compass we wouldn't have been able to do the art. We wouldn't have been able to do symmetry in art if we hadn't done it in maths.

In this interview, it becomes clear that the children were taking responsibility for their own learning, aware of how they learn best, what helps them to learn and what to do if they need help. It is interesting to note how much value they put on transferability, which should highlight to the teacher the importance of making learners aware of the relevance, not only of what they are learning, but also of the skills that they are using.

In another school pupils were asked to comment on the impact of the development of metacognition in their school. This is what they said:

The school has become more determined.
We are not afraid to take a challenge in our learning.
We are not afraid to make mistakes in lessons.
It has brought us closer together as a class.
I can't do it *yet* - we now learn from our mistakes.
We persevere more because of the language of learning.
This has allowed us to become braver when we make mistakes.
In August we didn't have the language of learning but now we are happier!
We are now becoming more positive and trying more.

Personal learning planning

When it comes to the time to set individual targets for learning it is hoped that the pupils will be able to set much more realistic and meaningful targets about *how* they learn, as opposed to comments about *what* they should learn. For example instead of saying, 'I need to be better at my tables', pupils might set targets such as 'I will try different ways to learn and understand multiplication'.

One way of assessing the impact of the suggestions in this book might be to compare the kind of targets and comments in the pupils' personal learning plans before and after the metacognitive approach is introduced. The hope is that through increased ownership and understanding of the learning process, PLPs and targets will become much more meaningful: less likely to be something the child (and their parents) see as a record of what they have not managed, and more likely to be a celebration of where they are on their learning journey and a record of achievable next steps that the child feels ownership of and also understands how to achieve.

Observations

It may be possible to gauge progress simply by observing the pupils as they go about their learning. In particular, one would be looking out for signs that they are able to use the language of learning as they go about their business. They should be able to try different strategies when they find the learning challenging, and above all they should have a positive, can-do attitude towards their learning.

It may be that you set each class some practical problem-solving challenge to complete in groups. By observing the way they go about the task, and possibly through discussing it with them afterwards, you might find evidence of their understanding of the different learning processes that they are able to use and of the kind of mindset they have. There are examples of this kind of activity in Chapter 8.

Discussions

It is possible to evaluate progress through some class discussions about learning in general, or through the *what makes a good learner* type activities (as discussed in Chapters 7 and 9). The teacher can find out a great deal simply by asking the class to talk about the skills they are aware of that help them with their work. The responses will enable the teacher to judge where the pupils are in terms of their metacognition and understanding of the language of learning. With time and opportunity to develop the things suggested in this book the pupils should be able to talk confidently about how they learn and be able to explain what they can do to work out how they, in particular, can *learn best*.

Attainment

There is also the more formal evidence of attainment. It might be that some significant progress can be found in the attainment of the pupils involved in this work on metacognition.

However, it might be difficult to prove that such an improvement is due only to the metacognitive approach. The range of interventions and scaffolding ideas in this book taken together will inevitably have some positive impact on attainment whether metacognition is a good idea or not.

It is also important to stress that this initiative is less about knowledge and curriculum success and more about attitude, mindset and transferable learning skills. Therefore one should be wary of how success is measured.

Assessing impact

When assessing impact we first of all need to consider what success would look like. The learning skills, attitudes and use of language would need to be evaluated, as well as the pupils' approaches towards learning in groups and independently. A short list of things to look out for would be:

- How well are pupils able to think and talk about how they learn?
- How much responsibility do they take for their own learning?
- How well can they talk about their own learning attitudes, skills and dispositions?
- How aware are they of their own strengths and learning needs?
- How open are they to working together and supporting others in their learning?
- How resilient are they when faced with new challenges?
- How willing are they to experiment with new approaches and strategies?
- How well do they understand how to get better at their learning?
- How aware are they of the transferable nature of their skills and dispositions?

Finding out the answers to these questions can be done in a variety of ways over a period of time. Some ideas for how to do this were explored in the section above on assessing progress, however, here it is important to look beyond the information we can gain from observations and discussions and think about how all of this input is manifest in formative and summative assessment evidence.

Sustaining development

Having introduced a metacognitive ethos in school and identified that it is having a positive impact on the skills, learning and attitudes of the learners, it is important to try to sustain this over a longer time period. We can do this through a number of strategies:

- maintain the approach as a focus in school development plans so that it remains high priority;
- school ethos;
- positive reinforcement and celebration of positive attitudes;
- informal learning conversations, reflective pit stops, any little steps along the way;
- assemblies;
- challenges;
- regular learning conversations and peer learning interactions;

- forward planning;
- reviews of teaching approaches;
- wall displays;
- sharing across cluster;
- links to high schools;
- learning councils/buddies;
- more focus on learning and less on content/curriculum.

Celebrating success

Of course one way to sustain the impact of metacognition on the learning in a class or school is to make sure that we take every opportunity to keep it high profile and to celebrate its success. We can do this through:

- assemblies;
- wall displays;
- websites;
- tweets;
- newsletters;
- sharing with parents;
- learning awards;
- sharing with the wider community.

Having the language of learning more focused and visible will help to maintain an awareness of the value attached to the metacognitive approach. Sharing words, pupils' work and above all the reflections of the learners about *how they learn* would also be a valuable way to celebrate their successes. This could be displayed on walls in the school as well as on the school website and in newsletters that are sent home.

It may be that assemblies are used, not only to have a focus on particular learning vocabulary and dispositions, but also to celebrate the work and attitudes of classes or individuals. Each class in the school could take turns to present an assembly on a specific learning process or approach. This would involve a focus on the process across all learning, leading to a compilation or portfolio of learning activities that benefitted from the target process, both in and outside school.

Celebration of metacognition in assembly might manifest itself in something as simple as the language that is used to describe success. For example, instead of awarding certificates in assembly for good work or for achieving Level 2, the language used should focus more on the skills used, the transferable learning skills such as for *organising and managing* your project, or for *making connections* and *using other learning* to tackle a new challenge.

Having a pupil learning council whose members are, as part of their remit, responsible for identifying and celebrating good learning is also a good way to find and celebrate success. Such a forum enables the pupils themselves to feel ownership of the approach and benefit from their creative ideas for sharing and celebrating success.

Summary and key points

In this chapter we have explored ways of moving from thinking and talking about how we learn, to thinking and talking about how we learn *best*. We have considered ways of making our learning more explicit and setting an ethos where we share our learning approaches and try new ways to do things, in order to explore how each of us can *learn best*. We also considered ways of assessing the progress and impact of these initiatives in a class or in a whole school.

Next steps for the reader

If you have managed to work through some of the suggestions in this book for raising awareness about how we learn, through learning conversations, exploring the language of learning, etc., you may be ready to shift the focus more on to how we learn best. You might want to consider some kind of audit to gauge where you are up to and to try to ascertain how well the pupils respond to the questions listed above in the section 'Assessing Impact'.

You might also explore further opportunities for involving pupils in thinking and talking and making decisions about how they learn.

Further reading on the work of Hattie and Dweck might also be a worthwhile next step.

References

Dweck, C. (2012) *Mindset: How You Can Fulfil Your Potential*. New York: Ballantine Books.
Hattie, J. (2011) *Visible Learning for Teachers: Maximizing Impact on Learning*. London: Routledge.

Appendices

Resource bank

These appendices are intended as a bank of resources to be used by practitioners aiming to put the ideas from the book into practice. As the development of a metacognitive approach is an iterative process, there is no single order in which to organise these resources. Throughout the book, issues, ideas and strategies are revisited from multiple perspectives. On this basis, we have arrived at one logical grouping of resources and provide an index and this brief guide to using the resource bank, so that you are able to navigate your way successfully to the resources you require. The appendices are referred to by name and number throughout the text.

1 Introducing metacognition in your school

In this section you will find resources intended for use when the metacognitive approach is introduced into school or a class. There are questionnaires for pupils and adults through which it is possible to gain a pre-project snapshot of attitudes, understanding and behaviours in relation to learning. The other resources here are all tried and tested ways in which to bring an initial focus on the language of learning and the concept of thinking about how we learn. The instructions for the learning carousel activity discussed in Chapter 3 can also be found here.

2 Resources for learning conversations

The resources here support learning conversations, learning pit stops and opportunities to stop, reflect and talk about learning. There are a variety of lists of questions and prompts for learning conversations. It is better to vary the prompts for discussion so that the focus remains on thinking and talking about recent learning.

3 Resources for profiling the language

It is not possible to talk about learning without the vocabulary. We need to move children from a basic vocabulary of learning to a wider one so that they have the language necessary to explore the nuances and differences in their approaches to learning. It is crucial to the whole process that there is a shared understanding of the language used and what it means in this learning context. In this section of the appendices, we offer some examples of how to profile a word so that everyone involved understands what it means in the context of their learning. This is also an opportunity to explore contexts when the word has another meaning. The model used here can be adapted for use with any target learning process.

4 Resources for staff development

The resources here are designed to be used by staff during INSET sessions to introduce and embed a metacognitive approach to learning. A set of guidance notes for looking at the approach from the perspective of learning in maths is included. There are also sample activities for teachers to try both with their peers and subsequently in the classroom with the pupils.

5 Resources for the language of learning

This section includes a variety of resources that contain the language of learning. The meta-learning word structure is a useful tool for introducing the language to pupils and staff as well as a means of recording processes and a stimulus for conversation about learning. The meta-learning word progression sets out the language that might be used at different stages in the school and has formed the basis for the focus processes and language of the practical Chapters 5–8.

6 Other resources

This section includes photocopiable resources that you may wish to use in the classroom.

Appendices

Resource index

Resource index

1 Introducing metacognition in your school

Language of learning questionnaire for teachers and classroom support staff

Date:

Part 1: The children as learners

	Yes	No
Do they ever think about their learning?		
Do they talk to anyone about their learning?		

	Please write your answers below
If so, who do they talk to?	
What do you think the children know about how they learn?	
Do you think the children know why it might it be good to talk to someone about their learning?	
Who might the children choose to talk to about their learning?	
How would the children know if they were good at learning?	
How would you know how the children *feel* about their learning?	
Do the children know who would help them if they found the learning too easy or too hard? Who?	

Do the children know what kind of things they could do to help themselves learn more easily?	

Part 2: Adults as learners

	Please write your answers below
How often do you think about your learning?	
Who do you talk to about your learning?	
Who might be interested to talk to you about learning?	
How do you *feel* about your own learning?	
How do you know if you are good at learning?	
Who would help you if you wanted help with learning?	
What kind of things could you do to assist your learning?	

Language of learning questionnaire for older learners

Meta listeners project

Date:

Do you ever think about your learning?	
Do you talk to anyone about your learning?	
If yes, who do you talk to about your learning?	

What do you know about how you learn?
Why might it be good to talk to someone about your learning?

How do you feel about your learning?

Who might be interested to talk to you about learning?

How would you know if you were good at learning?

What do you do if you find the learning too easy or too hard?

What kind of things could you do to make learning better for you in class?

Teacher notes for the meta-learning audit sheet (see Appendix 5.1)

In order for pupils to begin to engage with the 'language of learning and thinking', it is useful to make the appropriate vocabulary much more explicit. Appendix 5.1, the meta-learning audit sheet, is designed to be used by pupils but can also be used by the school staff as part of training in this approach. In this document we offer one way in which to use the sheet with pupils to increase familiarity with target vocabulary.

Suggested structure

The class teacher should work through the sheet with the class, providing examples of their own thinking and inviting the pupils to volunteer their own answers.

The lesson I am thinking of is:

reading	writing	maths	project	art
drama	gym	music	group work	health

It is first necessary to have a specific focus for the discussion and make sure that everyone is thinking of the same lesson. It will be best to choose a recent lesson, for example *a recent writing session*.

1 Before I got started on the task, the learning and thinking I was doing was:

wondering	exploring	thinking	testing	trying out
guessing	choosing	deciding	suggesting	estimating

It is important here to model the process by using think alouds:

'Now I'm thinking, at the start of the lesson, were we *exploring*? Yes we were thinking – we were thinking how to show that the main character was scared and unsure. What about *testing*? Were we testing anything out?'

It is not essential to do this for every single word, but the discussion about the words does enable pupils to better understand what they mean in the context of learning and thinking.

Once a few have been modelled the pupils should highlight the words which they feel best describe their learning and thinking for this particular lesson.

The teacher could then ask:

'Who highlighted *guessing*? Tell me more about that'.
'Who put *suggesting*? Tell me more.'

2 During the task the learning and thinking I was doing was:

trying	thinking	concentrating	taking care	using my plan
working out	problem-solving	trying different ways	making connections	remembering other learning

This section looks at the next part of the lesson. The teacher might need to talk about the distinction between before, during and after the lesson. Again, it is important to model, to use think alouds to explore the kind of learning and thinking going on.

Again the pupils should be asked to complete their own sheet after the teacher has modelled the process. The teacher could repeat the discussion about what they highlighted. It is important to reassure them that it is quite likely that they will all use and highlight different skills.

3 At the end of the task the learning and thinking I was doing was:

remembering	checking	considering	noticing	improving
redrafting	showing others	adding more detail	making changes	making connections

Repeat as for 1 and 2 above.

4 My feelings during this learning were:

confident	anxious	excited	bored	enthusiastic
happy	frustrated	confused	relaxed	curious

This next section is to do with the feelings of the learner before, during and after the lesson. The teacher should model their own feelings and then get the children to select and discuss their feelings. Allow them to highlight as many as they think apply. It might be useful to allow them to add any other words of their own.

5 Is there anything else that you would like to tell us about your own learning and thinking?

This again should be modelled before inviting the children to write something, e.g.

'I found this easier than I expected.'
'I had to ask for help today.'
'I wish I had a better imagination.'

Follow up

After this introductory session, the pupils should be given the opportunity to use the same structure to share another learning experience of their own choice in the same way.

Appendix 1.3

Language

The sheet can be adapted for use with children of all ages and can be reduced to include the learning vocabulary that is currently part of the class or school focus. The meta-learning word progression sheet (Appendix 5.3) serves as a useful guide to appropriate vocabulary.

Caution

It would be unfortunate if the activity became a 'tick-box' experience rather than an enabling opportunity to talk about thinking and learning.

Card sort

Metacognition focus words

One way to use these cards is described in Appendix 4.2.

Yellow cards

reading	writing	maths	project	art
drama	gym	music	group work	health

Blue cards

wondering	exploring	thinking	testing	trying out
guessing	choosing	deciding	suggesting	estimating

Green cards

trying	thinking	concentrating	taking care	using my plan

working out	problem-solving	trying different ways	making connections	remembering other learning
cooperating	being a good team member	sharing	considering others	supporting others

remembering	checking	considering	noticing	improving
redrafting	showing others	adding more detail	making changes	making connections

Purple cards

confident	anxious	excited	bored	enthusiastic
happy	frustrated	confused	relaxed	curious

reading	writing
drama	gym
maths	project
music	group work
art	health

wondering	exploring
guessing	choosing
thinking	deciding
testing	trying out
suggesting	estimating

This activity and resources were first printed in Tarrant, P. (2013) *Reflective Practice and Professional Development* (London: SAGE) and are reproduced with permission from SAGE Publications.

trying	thinking
working out	problem-solving
concentrating	taking care
trying different ways	making connections
using my plan	remembering other learning

cooperating	being a good team member
sharing	considering others
supporting others	

remembering	checking
redrafting	showing others
considering	noticing
adding more detail	making changes
improving	making connections

confident	anxious
happy	frustrated
excited	bored
confused	relaxed
enthusiastic	curious

This activity and resources were first printed in Tarrant, P. (2013) *Reflective Practice and Professional Development* (London: SAGE) and are reproduced with permission from SAGE Publications.

Thinking about how I learn

WHAT?   Describe *what* kind of learning and thinking you did. (Use the word bank to help you.)

Beginning:

During:

End:

HOW?   Describe *how* you did your thinking.

How did you go about your thinking?

What sort of things did you have to think about?

What helped you to do this?

What was your plan? How did you hope to work things out?

Appendix 1.6

WHY?   Evaluate your thinking.

- Was your thinking good? Why?
- Did you have a good plan (or strategy)?
- How could you improve your thinking next time?

Learning carousel

What makes a good learner?

Divide the class into six groups with poster paper at each group.

Each poster has one of the following questions written in the centre (you could choose four or six questions from these eight depending on the age and experience of your class):

1   What is learning?
2   What learning do we know we do?
3   Where do we learn?
4   How do we learn?
5   How do we talk about learning?
6   How do we learn best?
7   How can our learning be transferred?
8   How can we help others to learn?

Each group has a pen and gets around 3–4 minutes to write down their ideas on the poster in response to the question.

After 4 minutes or so move each poster round to the next group and get them to look at the comments already listed. It is a good idea to give each group a different coloured pen so you can see which ideas come from each group. You might also ask each group to read each comment and put a tick or cross to indicate whether or not they agree, or a question mark if they don't understand the comment.

Next give them 3–4 minutes to add their own thoughts to the question.

Repeat this so that each group tackles at least three of the poster questions. Generally three is enough to generate enough data to work on before children lose interest or feel that everything they would have said has already been said.

See Chapter 3 for suggested responses and follow up to this carousel.

2 Resources for learning conversations

Good listening

Learning to be an interviewer

The aim of this demonstration lesson is the development of skills to support learning conversations. It requires two adult demonstrators to model the role of interviewer/interviewee.

Instructions for teacher/demonstrators

1   Model some features of an interview where the interviewer asks a few questions about Edinburgh as a holiday destination. Do this as well as you can.
2   Ask the pupils what was done well in the interview and what not so well.
3   Repeat, this time doing it badly.
     The interviewer will demonstrate some bad habits:
     • interrogative style, too many rapid-fire questions
     • too much talking about themselves instead of listening to speaker
     • ignoring responses to questions and moving on to next question anyway
     • poor body language, disinterested (yawning, not looking)
     • negative reactions and comments.

     The interviewee will demonstrate some poor responses:

     • no responses
     • single word responses
     • not listening, answering own questions
     • keeps talking with no pause for interaction.

4   Pupils are then asked to discuss with a partner what was good and what was bad about each character's contribution.
5   From the ensuing discussion, success criteria for a good interview can be established.
6   Model an interview where things do not go well. Ask the class to use the success criteria as a guide to identify how the interviewer might improve their approach.
7   Pupils then pair up and host an interview on the subject of one of my favourite holidays.
8   Pupils swap partners and repeat as before, but take on the other role this time
9   Share feedback on the experience, good and bad. What were the good questions and approaches? How were challenges overcome?
10   As a class, compile some good questions. Consider also questions to do with feelings.
11   Ask the pupils to work in pairs and imagine that one of them is a famous chat show host and the other is a very famous celebrity. Conduct an interview.
12   Ask pupils to swap roles and repeat.

13 Encourage the pairs to stop and talk through what they have done, using the following prompts:
   a) Try to recall the whole session in order.
   b) Think about what you did, how you felt.
   c) What you might have learned about yourself, about someone else.
   d) Ask the whole class to share some of these recollections.

It can be helpful to have some starter questions to use as prompts, but it is important that everyone knows that they are just for when the interview dries up and they are not a list that has to be worked through. It should be made clear that it is better to formulate a question that relates to the previous answer.

Edinburgh questions

1 Do you like Edinburgh?
2 Do you come here often?
3 How many times have you been here?
4 Is it nicer than Glasgow?
5 Why do you come here?
6 What do you like about it?
7 What is your favourite part of Edinburgh?
8 Why do you like it?
9 What is the most memorable thing you have done here?
10 If you were recommending it to a friend what would you say about it?
11 Is there anything that you don't like about it?
12 How does it make you feel when you are here?
13 Is there anything else you can share with us about your experiences in Edinburgh?

Favourite holiday questions

1 Can you try to think of a favourite holiday you have had and tell me something about it?
2 Where did you go?
3 When was this?
4 Who was there?
5 Why would you say it was one of your favourites?
6 How did you feel when you were there?
7 What was the best thing about it?
8 If there had to be one thing that you had to change, what would it be?

Peer learning interactions

Work with a partner. Decide who is to be facilitating and who is to be thinking and talking about how they have been learning.

The facilitator will ask some of the questions below. The person listening to the questions should think carefully about their answers and should try to provide as much detail as they can.

Remember: You need to think about how you have been learning, what strategies you have used and what ideas you have about getting better in your learning.

Possible questions to ask

1   Think about a lesson you can remember from this week. Choose one that sticks in your mind for any reason, especially if it helps us to talk about how you have been learning.
2   Can you tell me why you have chosen this particular lesson?
3   What kind of learning were you doing? What skills were used?
4   How well did this go?
5   Were there any difficulties or challenges?
6   Can you tell me more?
7   If you were doing this again what would you do differently?
8   What would you try to keep doing?
9   Can you think of how this learning might be transferred to other areas of the curriculum?
10 Can you think of how this learning might be transferred to things you do out of school?
11 Can you think of anything or anyone that could help you to be better at this learning?
12 Is there anything else you want to tell me about this lesson?

Tell me about ....

What was it that ....

Have you ever ....

Do you always ....

Couldn't you have ....

Why didn't you ....

Would you ....

What did you ....

Can you remember ....

Questions to promote thinking about learning

1 Tell me about something you have been learning recently.
2 What did you learn?
3 How did you learn it?
4 What skills did you use?
5 Who helped you?
6 How successful were you?
7 How do you know?
8 What would you have done if you were stuck?
9 What are your next steps?
10 How will you do this?
11 Have you done this kind of learning in any other lesson?
12 How did this learning make you feel? Why?
13 How will this learning help you in the future?
14 Was there anything about the skills involved in your learning that might help you in other learning?
15 Which elements of this learning will be useful in the future? Why?

3 Resources for profiling the language

Deciding/choosing

Organise the class into groups.

1 Ask each group to think of situations where they have to make a decision, inside or outside of school, e.g.
   - choosing to play at the water or the sand;
   - whether to have a school lunch or a packed lunch;
   - whether to wear a coat at breaktime;
   - whether to watch TV or go out to play.
2 Ask each group to think about the things that they have to do and the skills that they need to use in order to choose/make the decision, e.g.
   - How do you decide?
   - What do you think about?
   - What 'factors' do you consider?
   - What helps you to decide?
   - What skills do you need?
3 Ask them to set out some instructions for making a decision about
   - which game to play at playtime;
   - which information to include in a report;
   - what to paint in an art lesson;
   - who you can work well with;
   - how to present your work;
   - what order to do your work in.
4 For example:
   How to decide which laptop to buy:
   a) Think about why you need a laptop and make a list of what you need it to do.
   b) Work out how much you can afford to pay.
   c) Do some research about both options. Find out as much as you can about each laptop, its price and its capabilities.
   d) Make two lists: write down reasons for and against buying each one.
   e) Take one list away. Imagine you have to buy the laptop you wrote about in the remaining list. Consider how you feel.
   f) Now swap lists and repeat this. How would you feel?
   g) Other things you might do if you are still unsure:
      - ask your parents/teacher;
      - ask your friends;
      - read some reviews;
      - go back to consider 1 above.
5 Link the skills explored here to the language of learning and the metacognitive work done about other skills and dispositions.

Remembering

1   Start with an activity that involves remembering: learning a new trick, a song, some facts or a series of numbers like tables. With younger learners it might mean simply playing Kim's Game.

Learning a song: Go over one line, repeat it back. Go over the next line, repeat both. Go over another line repeat all three.
Kim's Game: Look at the objects. Are there any links? Do they have anything in common? Are there objects that begin with the same initial? Will that help you to remember them?

2   When the activity is over ask the learners to think back about what they have just been doing:
   • Think through what you just did. What did we do to help you to remember?
   • How did that make it easier?
   • What are the key learning words here?

Possible responses:

   • Repeat the activity.
   • Look for patterns and clues.
   • Link to other things we know.

3   What other ways do you know that help you to remember things?

The teacher might make a list on the board, or pupils can write ideas on Post-its to bring out to a display. If this is done as a whole school assembly then each class can be challenged to contribute ideas to a whole school noticeboard. Then if there are some good ideas on the board the pupils who posted them can be invited to go into another class and teach them their special way of remembering.

The main point here is that the word *remember* is profiled. There is a shared understanding of what it means. Strategies for remembering are shared and explored. Pupils are invited to try different strategies in order to establish what works best for them in a given situation.

This is learning about learning and each individual has the opportunity to find out what works best for them.

Appendix 3.3

Trying

What does it mean to try?

This word is used within varying combinations of words. It is worth exploring the different things meant by the word 'try' and how the meaning varies when paired with another word such as 'out' or 'hard'.

Possible meanings:

- make an attempt/guess
- test something out
- not giving up
- having a strategy
- having a plan
- doing my best
- experimenting
- having a go and seeing what happens
- being brave to try something
- not being afraid to fail
- not being distracted or put off.

Look at the various meanings and decide what you mean as a class when you are focusing on *trying*.

Is this different to *trying out*?

How does the meaning change when you use *try hard*?

As there are multiple interpretations, it is important that the class (and school) agree on the meaning that they have. In the language progression sheets, each time *try* is included we have attempted to qualify try with another word to make our meaning clear. *Try out* vs *try hard* vs *try again*. It may be appropriate to use a synonym instead. See how the word is profiled in Chapters 5–8 and how it occurs in the Meta-learning Audit Sheet (Appendix 5.1).

Making connections

Making connections is a useful learning skill, but what does it mean, and how can we explore this with our learners?

It might be best approached through an activity where the learners experience it first. *Making connections* is something that teachers and pupils do all of the time; it's just that they do not necessarily realise it or have any time to reflect upon it in a metacognitive manner.

As a teacher the first step when introducing something new is generally activating prior knowledge. If the class are going to do a project on The Romans, the teacher may well begin by asking, 'What do we know about the Romans?' But a different approach might be: 'Today we are going to look at how people in the past lived and at some of the things they introduced that we still use today. In this project we will need to use lots of different skills. Let's begin by making a list of the skills we will need for a historical project'.

Possible responses:

> research, look up, read, discover, remember, take notes, write reports, draw, make, work together, cooperate, review, evaluate, etc.

It is unlikely that the class would actually volunteer the words *make connections* or *activate prior knowledge*. Therefore it might be valuable for the teacher to introduce these terms. It might go something like this:

This is going to be a historical topic. You have identified lots of learning skills that we will need. But think back to the last historical project we did, yes, The Vikings. Think of all of the activities we did. Think of the skills we needed. How many of those skills will help us here? Can we transfer any of our knowledge and skills?

Yes, a timeline would be valuable; we used one last time. Yes, the BBC website does have some good links to historical topics.

Think about the way we approached the topic on The Vikings. Can we adopt a similar approach here?

Yes, we might look at how the Romans came to be in our country, and at the kind of homes they build and what their way of life was like.

Do you see how making connections to other learning that we have done can help us to structure and organise our new learning? Think too about how we can use and develop lots of other learning skills. Don't forget to think about how you might also transfer these skills and approaches to other learning too.

Perhaps we won't divide our maths into the same categories, but sometimes a maths problem is easier to solve if we split the task up into sections in the same way as we are going to do here with our topic on The Romans.

Appendix 3.4

This example shows that a typical lesson or topic can be used to include and develop meta-cognition. You do not need to have a new lesson or create something specific in order to highlight and develop metacognition for the pupils. This meta-learning is more of a pedagogy than a subject. It should not really be about the activity, but about how you put it across and how you provide the opportunity to make the learning skills much more visible.

Structuring/organising

Whether you use the term *structure* or the term *organise* or both of them, it is important to unpack the meaning and identify when the skill is used. They are used interchangeably here, but we recommend deciding which term to use as a class and favouring that one, whilst being aware of synonyms that name the same process.

This is a learning word that is worth unpacking. There are many occasions when a pupil has to structure or organise their thoughts, ideas or activities. When setting out the learning intentions for a lesson it is important to draw attention to this skill. Part of this approach will involve some discussion about what this means, how to go about it, the process itself and the review of how it helped and the finished product.

- Introduce the term in a meaningful context.
- Invite some discussion about what it means to structure.
- Model some examples.
- Establish what it means to the class.
- Identify where in the learning it is necessary and why it is needed.
- Discuss how we might review afterwards how this has helped.

Example:

Teacher:	Today we will be writing a report on our visit to the museum. We have already created a mindmap of the many different things we did on the visit. But we can't just present them in any old random fashion! We will need to structure and organise the information. Why do you think we need to do that?
Pupil:	So that it is easy to understand.
Pupil:	So that the reader can see the most important information.
Pupil:	So we have the interesting bits and don't repeat things.
Teacher:	Good answers. So how might we structure this report?

Pupils would be given the opportunity to share ideas about how to structure and organise this report. These are then shared. Together teacher and class agree the criteria for a well-structured report.

Teacher:	Now that we know that it is important to structure our work and we have agreed how we are going to do this, can you see how important a learning skill *structuring and organising* is?
Teacher:	Who can think of other areas of school where we do this?
Child:	We do this in writing stories.
Child:	When we look at spelling patterns.

Child:	Sometimes in maths when we are handling data.
Teacher:	Who can think of situations out of school where structuring and organising are helpful?
Child:	When we are planning things we need to structure what to do first, second, etc.
Child:	Like when you go camping or put up a tent.
Child:	Yes and when you are trying to share information.
Teacher:	How can we find out how we might get better at organising our thoughts, ideas and activities?
Child:	We need to look at it carefully to see if it does the job well.

Pupils need to become aware of lots of different situations where they are using the skill of structuring and organising. The different ways of structuring information can be explored within meaningful contexts:

- Structuring thinking might be modelled through maths problems.
- In a gymnastics lesson they might need to think through the structure of a sequence they are performing.
- In art and design there will be a need to think through the organisation of their ideas and presentations.

It is important that the pupils see that putting things into an ordered structure and logical sequence has many benefits and many applications for learning.

Determined

Exploring learning dispositions during school assembly

1 Introduction in which the following ideas are developed:

- What does 'determined' mean?
- Can you think of examples?
- What does it look like? (This is tricky to articulate.)
- What does it sound like? (e.g. 'I can do this!', 'This won't beat me!', etc.)
- What does it feel like? (e.g. 'Hard work', 'Frustrating', 'Great when you make it!')
- Can you make connections with any learning you have had, inside or outside school? (e.g. learning to talk, walk, ride a bike, swim, ride a skateboard, etc.)
- How did it feel? In what way did you show your determination?
- Did it always work out? How do you feel when it doesn't work out?

You might introduce the word 'resilient' here, i.e. 'bouncing back', 'getting back up again'.

2 Tell a story of someone who is a good example of this quality, i.e. someone famous who overcomes many challenges could be an example of the word 'determined'.

- This week I want you all to try to be aware of times when you need to be determined – both in school and out of it!
- Come back and tell us what determination looks like for you and what it feels like.
- Perhaps you could make us some signs showing phrases about being determined, like the ones we heard in this assembly? (e.g. 'Don't give up!', 'I know I can do it', 'One more try!')

3 Arrange for the management team or school leader to visit to each class over the course of the week. Ask:

- What did you learn in assembly this week? (Have a coloured card with the word 'determined' written on it.)
- How did you learn this? (Write their ideas on card: it is likely they will offer words such as 'we listened', 'we thought', 'made connections', 'worked it out', 'remembered', etc.)
- How does it feel while you are being determined? Does it always work out?
- How do you feel when it doesn't work out?
- We think it would be a good idea to put these cards around the board to remind you of these learning words. Remember that these skills can be used for lots of learning both in and out of the classroom. Try to be aware of when you are using them. Tell your teacher when you think that you do.

- I will be back next week to hear about how you use these words. Perhaps you might add other words of learning to the display around the board, I do hope so!

4 Follow up

In another assembly or visit to class 'determination' can be re-visited. Pupils can share their experiences, further consolidating their understanding of this attitude to *learning*. Some focus on their *determined* phrases would be beneficial, and ownership can be shared by displaying these around school.

The emotive aspect should also be discussed:

- How did it feel?
- What happened when you thought you weren't going to make it? etc.

Examples from in and out of school should be explored so that they can begin to appreciate the transferable element of learning skills.

The word 'resilient' might be explored at this point too.

5 Exploring other learning dispositions

The above approach might be used to consider other dispositions.

Carousel exploring 'persevering' in our learning

Resources

- four large sheets of paper
- four different coloured marker pens.

Organisation

Write the following questions on the sheets of paper:

When have you had to persevere IN school?
When have you had to persevere OUT of school?
What helps you to persevere?
What does perseverance look like?
What does perseverance sound like?
What does perseverance feel like?

Organise the class into four to six groups depending on how many questions you want to include.
Remind them about this week's word and what it means.
Get some general examples from the class before starting the carousel.

Activity

Each group will have about 5 minutes to record their ideas on the large pieces of paper. After 5 minutes the sheets will move to another group. Here the group will tick anything they agree with, put a cross if they disagree, and a question mark against anything they don't understand. Then they will have 5 minutes to add their own ideas. Each group should have a different coloured pen. The pen should stay with the group all the time.
This is repeated until all groups have explored all questions.

Plenary

Finally there is a plenary where the posters are put on the wall and the teacher can summarise the general understanding of this week's word, its meaning to them, and the transferable element of this learning skill.

4 Resources for staff development

Introducing a metacognitive approach to learning in your school

1   Introduce the concept in a staff session.
    a)   Share some background information about metacognition.
    b)   Use the meta-learning audit sheet (Appendix 5.1) to get staff to consider the level of metacognition and the language of learning that they currently employ in their teaching.
    c)   Model the peer learning questions in terms of metacognition using the questions in Appendix 2.4.
    d)   Participants should use these questions to work with a partner to consider where they are now in terms of this approach. They should come up with ideas and suggestions about how to introduce a more explicit metacognitive approach in school, e.g. words that might be displayed to support pupils learning about learning, and the lessons or parts of lessons in which this might be done.
2   Introduce the concept with pupils.
    a)   The teacher models the thinking process with their class. (There are examples illustrating how to do this throughout this book and in Appendix 1.3.)
    b)   In pairs, pupils explore the questions on the pupil reflection sheet (Appendix 1.6) for a number of lessons.
3   Introduce the peer learning approach with a class (see Appendices 2.1 and 2.2).
    a)   Look at famous examples of interviewing (good and bad).
    b)   Get pupils to identify what makes a good/bad interviewer.
    c)   In pairs, pupils take turns to interview their partner on a topic, e.g. my best holiday, my best friend, my favourite book/movie/TV show.
    d)   Have a volunteer come out to model their interview skills. Teacher comments on who does most of the talking, which questions work best, the power of silence and patience as the person questioned stops to think before answering.
    e)   Pupils now conduct interactions where one child has to focus on a lesson they can remember where they found something difficult or challenging (see the question guide in Appendix 2.4).
4   Practise using the language of learning in class.
5   Practise using some sort of audit tool (e.g. Appendix 1.6, 2.4 or 5.1) more frequently, i.e. once a week.
6   Develop skills for interviewing in pairs in your own class before moving on to work with pupils at a similar age and stage from another class.
7   Develop so that your class have peer learning interactions with pupils from a different age and stage.
8   Develop Learning about Learning Teams in which there might be four or five pupils from different stages of the school who frequently meet in pairs or as a whole group to discuss learning and how they learn best.

Meta-learners introduction – card sort activity

We want pupils to be able to know and articulate a response to the four questions:

1 I learn best when ....
2 The kind of learning and thinking I am doing is ....
3 When learning is difficult I can ....
4 I know I've learnt well when ....

Activity for staff using the Card Sort: Metacognition Focus Words (Appendix 1.4) (working in groups of three)

1 Look first at the yellow cards:
   • Think of an area of the curriculum and a lesson that one of you has taught recently that was, for some reason, memorable.
   • In a couple of sentences write down what it was that you wanted the children to learn.
2 Next look at the blue learning cards:
   • Discuss which of these *kinds of learning* the pupils were engaged in. Choose up to four blue learning cards.
3 Look now at the green learning cards:
   • Discuss which *learning skills* the pupils were engaged in. Choose up to four green learning cards.
4 Think back to your lesson aims. Ask yourself:
   • Did you share with the children *what* they learnt?
   • Did you share with the children *how* they learnt?
   • Am I teaching in a way that encourages this kind of learning?
   • Am I making it clear to the pupils that they are developing these kinds of learning and these learning skills?
   • Would they benefit as learners if they had a better idea that these learning skills were part of the learning intentions?
   • If you did this activity with a group of pupils, what kind of questions might you ask when you looked at the cards they had selected?

Metacognition
Metacognition can be broken down into different categories:

• task awareness;
• strategy awareness;
• skills awareness;
• performance awareness;

This activity and resources were first printed in Tarrant, P. (2013) *Reflective Practice and Professional Development* (London: SAGE) and are reproduced with permission from SAGE Publications.

Appendix 4.2

- reflective awareness; and
- emotive awareness.

Task

- Choose at least two lessons to focus on over the next two weeks.
- Look at your learning intentions and see if there are opportunities to make the learning to learn more explicit.
- You might use the list and questions as a focus, or you might use the card activity, or you might have ideas of your own.
- Try flagging the learning at the beginning and end of the lesson.
- Keep a note of the elements that you choose as your focus.
- Keep a note of some of the pupil responses.
- You might, for example, highlight some of the things on the questions sheet to monitor the kind of things you manage to profile.

This activity and resources were first printed in Tarrant, P. (2013) *Reflective Practice and Professional Development* (London: SAGE) and are reproduced with permission from SAGE Publications.

A metacognitive focus on maths

Resources: metacognition focus words (see Appendix 1.4), blank cards, A3 copies of the two grids below.

The participants are organised into groups with flipchart paper on which to share their ideas. Ask the groups to explore:

1 Maths – what is it? Can we divide it into elements?
The possible answers might include:

- number;
- shape;
- measure;
- mental;
- problem solving.

2 Each of these elements require certain skills and dispositions. Can you list these for the element you have been given?
The possible answers might include:

- listening;
- thinking;
- remembering;
- problem solving, etc.

3 Now look at the metacognition focus words (see Appendix 1.4). Which of these apply to your maths element?
Are there any words 'missing'?

4 Next think about transferable skills. Where else in maths are these skills used?
Where else in school are these skills used?
Where out of school are they used? Make connections.

Responses could be recorded onto the following grid:

In maths	In school	Beyond school

5 How can we help pupils to see the relevance of these skills and approaches, not just in maths, but in all of their learning?
How else can we share these words and the links to other learning?

Appendix 4.3

And who can help you?

Ideas could be recorded onto the following grid:

What can you do?	What can the learning council do?
What can the pupils in your class do?	What can other people in and out of school do?

6 Plan three things you might do with your learning council to get things started.

This session can end here with a plenary. You might also model metacognition by asking the participants to list on exit Post-its the skills they have had to use during this session.

A follow-up session could be designed around the sharing of ideas that each learning council has developed as a result of the session. A similar session could be developed with a focus on a different curriculum area.

Exploring learning challenges

Step 1

1 Organise participants into groups and allocate each group a different curricular area as its focus.
2 Ask:
   - What is sometimes difficult in this subject?
   - What are the challenges to successful learning?

   Each group writes their responses on a poster.
3 Move the posters around so that each group gets to think about a different curricular area for the next question.
4 Ask:
   - How might we overcome these challenges?
   - What skills and dispositions might we need?

   Move posters on again to get more ideas.
5 Collect in the posters and display them on the wall.

Step 2 (this could happen on another day)

1 Collate the common responses from the posters.
2 Which skills apply for different curricular areas?
3 Are there some skills that are unique to a particular area?
4 Are there skills/strategies that will help in different areas?
5 Link this discussion to transferable learning skills.
6 Use these words as a focus for exploring metacognition.
7 Link these words and the pupils' strategies to Lexi the Learner (see Appendix 4.5).

Lexi the learner

1   Do the 'What makes a good learner?' carousel (see Appendix 1.7 or follow the instructions in Appendix 4.4).
2   Filter results to exclude behaviour descriptors.
3   Create a class version of the perfect learner:
  - Draw around a child and call the character something unisex like 'Lexi Learner'.
  - Get the class to write words around this character to reflect how a good learner would think (inside the frame) and act (outside).
4   Use Lexi as a reference point so that when children are embarking on a task the teacher can say things like:

Teacher:	Today we are looking at some new spelling words. Now who can tell me what Lexi might be thinking when faced with a remembering task?
Child:	Look carefully.
Child:	Listen.
Child:	Think.
Teacher:	Yes, Lexi would say that you need to *look carefully*, *listen* and *think* about other work you have done that might help you here.
	Lexi might also say that we need to go over some of the *strategies* we have already learned for *working things out*, and for *remembering*.
Teacher:	Oh you are stuck? Well, what do you think Lexi would do in this situation?
	Lexi would tell you to *look carefully* at what you were asked to do. Lexi might also say *think* about where you might have come across something like this before. Words like *don't give up*, and *resilience* might be used, don't you think?

5 Resources for the language of learning

Meta-learning audit sheet

The lesson I am thinking of is:

reading	writing	maths	project	art
drama	gym	music	group work	health

1 Before I got started on the task, the learning and thinking I was doing was:

wondering	exploring	thinking	testing	trying out
guessing	choosing	deciding	suggesting	estimating

2 During the task the learning and thinking I was doing was:

trying	thinking	concentrating	taking care	using my plan
working out	problem-solving	trying different ways	making connections	remembering other learning

3 At the end of the task the learning and thinking I was doing was:

remembering	checking	considering	noticing	improving
redrafting	showing others	adding more detail	making changes	making connections

4 My feelings during this learning were:

confident	anxious	excited	bored	enthusiastic
happy	frustrated	confused	relaxed	curious

5 Is there anything else that you would like to tell us about your own learning and thinking?

Guidance on the use of this sheet can be found in Appendix 1.3. Other words from the meta-learning word progression sheet (Appendix 5.3) could be substituted.

Metacognition peer learning process map

Teacher Using the language of learning Asking the focus questions Modelling both questions and answers	Modelled
Pupils At first responding to teacher questions Later taking turns at 'being teacher' and Asking the questions of the class	Shared
Group Pupils in groups using the focus questions to explore 'how they learn'	Guided
Partner With a learning partner having a more in depth look at learning on a weekly basis	Guided
Individual Pupils being encouraged to think about how they learn more often	Independent
Extension Pupils visit peers from other classes and conduct metacognitive peer learning interactions	Reflection

Appendix 5.3

Meta-learning word progression sheet

Learning words for the nursery

looking	listening	feeling
guessing	choosing	deciding
thinking	remembering	sharing
taking turns	wondering	keep trying
trying out	finding out	using imagination

Learning words for the early years
Learning words for the nursery plus these below:

trying different ways	being a good team member	exploring
remembering other learning	showing others	testing
suggesting	estimating	working out
taking care	solving problems	cooperating

Learning words for the middle years
Learning words for the nursery and early years plus these below:

testing	checking	planning
expressing feelings and thoughts	noticing	redrafting
making connections	improving	considering others
concentrating	supporting	using other learning
looking for patterns	revising/retrying	estimating

Learning words for the upper years

looking/observing	listening	feeling	guessing
choosing	deciding	thinking	remembering
sharing	taking turns	wondering	keep trying
trying out	trying different ways	finding out	using imagination

© 2016, *Metacognition in the Primary Classroom*, P. Tarrant and D. Holt, Routledge.

being a good team member	exploring	remembering other learning	showing others
suggesting	testing	solving problems	working out
taking care	checking	cooperating	noticing
planning	improving	redrafting	supporting
expressing feelings and thoughts	explaining thoughts and opinions	justifying choices, suggestions and opinions	making connections
considering others	concentrating	using own plan	predicting
planning ahead	finding evidence	applying other learning	

6 Other resources

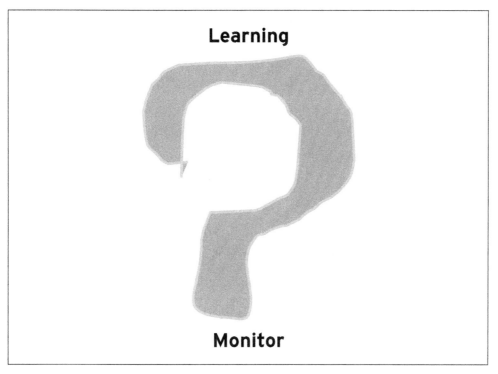

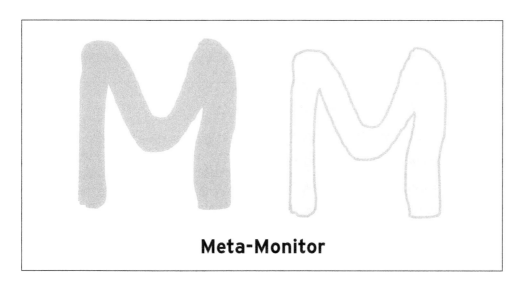

Crossing the swamp

Resources

- large open space (gym or outside)
- hoops
- mats
- cones as markers for swamp.

Learning intentions

The learning intentions for this activity are PE based but also include collaborative learning and metacognition:

- I can work together with others to find a solution.
- I can improve my range of physical skills (PE).
- I can choose, adapt and apply physical movement skills and strategies with control to achieve a goal (PE).
- I can explain how I have set out to achieve a goal.

Metacognition focus (any of the following processes)

working out	working together	making decisions
thinking	listening to others	remembering other learning
planning ahead -predicting what might happen	trying out	making improvements

Activity

This is a practical activity, best done outside or in a big space like a gym hall. The class is divided into groups. Each group has three small hoops or mats as stepping stones. There is a clearly defined swamp zone in the space. The challenge for each group is to get their whole team and all of the equipment across the swamp without touching the floor. The swamp is too wide to jump across or to throw the stepping stones across. The group will need to discover the best way to work as a team in order to get across. There is emphasis on collaborative skills and on applying what they already know about passing objects and moving safely.

This lesson demands responsiveness from the teacher, who will be supporting the pupils throughout to work as a team and to focus on *how* they will achieve the goal and solve the problem. It might be useful to look at the target metacognitive processes, or to get the pupils to identify them, so that the pupils are aware that the way to achieve the task is to think carefully about how they will do so. The teacher may need to stop the whole class or interact with individual groups if they see opportunities to explore metacognition regarding *how we learn best*.

Reflection

It is important to follow up the activity with a learning conversation or peer learning interaction. See elsewhere in the book for sample questions and approaches.

Newspaper technology

Resources

- sheets of newspaper rolled tightly into rods and taped - five or six per group (creating these can be part of the activity).

Learning intentions (including for metacognition)

- I can work as part of a team to solve a problem.
- I can apply my learning and skills to a problem.
- I can revise and improve my plans to make something work.
- I can explain what skills I have used and how I have solved a problem.

Metacognition focus (any of the following processes)

looking (observation)	listening	thinking
remembering	making connections	working collaboratively
guessing/predicting	trying out working out	improving - retrying (revise and improve)

If the pupils are new to thinking about how they learn, it will be necessary for the teacher to use these words explicitly and draw the pupils' attention to them as they progress through the task. With a class who have more experience of the language of learning, there may be more emphasis on getting the pupils to identify the metacognition.

Activity

The task involves using newspaper rods. It will be necessary to begin by teaching the basic rolling technique before starting this activity. A pencil is used to begin the rolling of the newspaper sheet into a tightly rolled tube. This is taped to prevent it unrolling and then the pencil retrieved. Each group will need at least five newspaper rods each.

The task for each group is to use the newspaper rods to construct a bridge capable of supporting the weight of the teacher. (Or if you feel that this is pushing it too much, substitute something more appropriate from the classroom!) The groups are only allowed their newspaper rods and some extra tape.

Before

Before the pupils begin the task they are told to revisit the skills they have discussed and developed in previous practical group tasks. They should share what they feel were their strengths and challenges. They should make sure that they are aware of their target skills to work on today.

During

They are given a fixed time to complete the task and are reminded to keep the skills they are using in mind as they go. There will be a learning skills list on the classroom wall for reference. At the end of the task there can be a plenary which enables the groups to discuss what they did, what they learned, and which skills they used or developed.

Reflection

It is important to follow up the activity with a learning conversation or peer learning interaction. See elsewhere in the book for sample questions and approaches.

Reading the impossible

Resources

- copies of the 'Reading the Impossible' text.

Learning intentions (including for metacognition)

- I am learning about how to make sense of an unfamiliar text.
- I am learning about how to describe the skills and strategies I need to make sense of a text.
- I am learning about how to make connections to other learning.

Metacognition focus (any of the following processes)

looking (observation)	thinking	making connections
guessing	trying out	solving problems

Activity

Reading the impossible
In'st it isetnreintg taht wehn the lterets in a wrod are in the wonrg oderr yuo can aulaclty slitl uesdtannrd waht yur'oe rdnaieg.
Htis mkeas you tinhk aoubt how yuo raed as wlel as wtah you raed.
It dseno't mttaer in waht oderr the lterets in a wrod are yuo can laenr mroe aoubt teh srtageits yuo use to wrok out ufmarialin wrods.

1   In your group try to read the text.
2   While you are involved in the task try to be aware of the skills you are using in the process.
3   At the end of the task make a list of these skills and strategies.
4   Each group should discuss how they tackled the challenge and the skills they used.
5   Now each group should share their ideas about these skills and strategies and how they might be useful in other situations (transferable learning).

Reading pictures

Resources

- large picturebook.

Learning intentions (including for metacognition)

The learning intentions for this activity are to learn about learning and to read a picture. This might be explored and expressed more specifically as:

- I can *describe* the learning skills I am using in this task.
- I can *find information* in a text/picture.
- I can *make decisions* about the text.
- I can *justify my decisions* with evidence.

Metacognition focus (any of the following processes)

looking	making connections	explaining and justifying thoughts
working out	using imagination	finding evidence

Activity

1 At the start of the lesson the teacher will ask the pupils to think about reading:

Teacher:	What learning skills do you need to read?
Pupil:	Looking, concentrating, making connections.
Pupil:	Thinking, considering, asking questions, using your imagination.

Pupils are asked to use a chart to plot any learning skills they use during the lesson (see Appendix 5.1).

Teacher:	Tell me what you can see?
Pupil:	A boy in red shoes.
Teacher:	What else?
Pupil:	A tree with a face in it!
Teacher:	Well done, you *looked carefully* and you *made a connection* to something familiar.

Pupil:	I can see a basket in his hand and he's going into the woods.
Pupil:	Yes like Little Red Riding Hood – but it's a boy!
Teacher:	Well done, you have *explained* what you could see and provided *evidence* from the text. You have also shown how you can make *connections* between what you can see and what you already know.
Teacher:	What else can you notice?
Pupil:	I can see a … a shadow and it's a bit like Red Riding Hood!
Teacher:	Yes it does a bit doesn't it? Well done, you *looked* carefully and used your *imagination* to *work out* what you thought.

2 Next the teacher models how to 'look' at a picture.

3 Having asked the questions and explicitly modelled the identification of the learning skills for the class, the next step is for the pupils to investigate a text/picture of their own.

Each group is given a new picture to look at and they are challenged to annotate the picture to show what decisions they can make about it – for example what they can see, what do they think it means, and what evidence can they offer to support these decisions. This can be done using Post-its in three colours: red for what they think, yellow for evidence in the picture, green for evidence in the text.

4 After a while the pupils are stopped for a meta-learning pit stop.

Teacher:	Let's share something about how we are learning.
	Who can tell us which learning skills they have been using?

5 Once pupils have shared these they then share the product of their investigations of the text/picture. The role of the teacher here is to articulate *the way the pupils learned*: a focus on words such as yes you *looked*, you *used your imagination*, you made *connections*, etc. enables these skills to be more explicit and heightens the pupils' awareness of *how* they are learning.

In school:	
Teacher:	Where else in school do you use these skills?
Pupil:	In music we have to *concentrate* and *read* the notes.
Pupil:	In language we have to *read* the words and try to *understand* what they are saying.
Pupil:	In topic work we have to *find information* and *provide evidence* about it.

Out of school:

Teacher: What about out of school? Where might you need these skills that you have been using today?

Pupil: When we play football we have to *listen* to the coach and *remember* our instructions.

Pupil: At Brownies we have to *look for clues* when we are playing wide games.

Pupil: On my computer game I need to *concentrate* and *find patterns* to get points.

Teacher: Yes, so you see that the skills we have been using today are useful not just for this reading task, but also for lots of other subjects where we learn in school. They are also useful out of school whether it is to do with school, sport or playing with your friends.

6 Having identified the words that describe *how* they learned the teacher then asks:
It is very important to identify these learning skills and make explicit the transferable nature of them. Helping pupils to realise that the skills have some relevance and use beyond school, in their own leisure activities, does help them to see that the skills are important for them – not just for the teacher!

How to learn *better*

This is the next step, and it might not be one to take at this point in the pupils' development. It is not enough simply to identify how we are learning. We need at some point to have a focus on each of these transferable learning skills and to try to develop and improve how we use them.
7 At the end of a lesson like this it might simply be enough to say:

Choose one of these skills that you used today that you think you are good at.
Tell your learning partner what that skill is and why you think you are good at it.
Try to provide evidence to support what you say.

This self-assessment activity helps to consolidate the metacognition for the learners, not only the person telling their partner but also the person listening and asking questions.
8 At this point the teacher might go on to say:

Choose one of these skills that you used today that you think you not so good at.
Tell your learning partner what that skill is and how you think you might get better at it.
Try to provide evidence to support what you say.

Powerful verbs

Resources

- pictures of scenes from stories which demonstrate actions
- word cards
- metacognition words on the classroom wall.

Learning intentions

- I can use power words to make my writing interesting.
- I can share my ideas and listen to the opinions of others.
- I know that using imagination and trying different ways are helpful in my learning.

Metacognition focus (any of the following processes)

exploring	sharing	taking turns	showing others
trying different ways	using imagination	remembering other learning	

Activity

1 Remind the class about prior work done in class on verbs.
2 In pairs or groups they are asked to come up with some interesting/powerful *doing* words.
3 After the introductory activities with the teacher, the children are given some pictures of scenes and word cards to create captions. They have to work in groups using word cards to build sentences that have an interesting or powerful verb. (Examples might be raced/rushed/crawled/wandered rather than went.) They will also have blank cards so that they can add more interesting words.
4 During the work the teacher should take opportunities for reflective pit stops.
5 Pupils could be asked to use a chart to plot any learning skills they use during the lesson (see Appendix 5.1).

Reflection

It is important to follow up the activity with a learning conversation or peer learning interaction. See elsewhere in the book for sample questions and approaches.

Index